WHO ARE THEY?

by

Margaret-Ellen Fry

First limited edition published by the author M.E. Fry
October 2004

Printed and bound by
Fineline Printing & Stationery Ltd,
23 Clwyd Street, Ruthin, Denbighshire,
LL15 1HH, North Wales

ISBN: 0-9548985-0-8

Computer editing by J.Rudkin

Illustrations by M.E.Fry

Cover design by K.E. & J. Pepperell/M.E.Fry

CONTENTS

ACKNOWLEDGEMENTS

This book would never have been written were it not for the unfailing support of my husband Ron who has mastered the complexities of a computer far better than I, and his sister Janet Rudkin who has had the patience of Job in typing, retyping and putting all these alterations into one CD for me. Without Ron's cooperation throughout 32 years of marriage in motoring me to investigations, I could never have become a field investigator, as I do not drive a car. My kind daughter-in-law Celia Costello for also taking me to various investigations, Conferences and proof-reading for me. Alan Hilton - hypnotist, physiotherapist, air pilot my friend and partner since 1976 in our team work of Abduction Victim Support. Timothy Good and Patricia Grant for their unfailing support, particularly in the case of Mrs Sage of Chatham. Helen and Mel Roberts owners of Solo Office Suppliers Shop, Abergele, North Wales for their continuous kindnesses over a period of years in helping me to produce this book. Also Marie Thomas for patiently proof reading. Last but not least, the late Desmond Leslie for telling me he would be delighted to write an Introduction for my book, and permitting me to extensively use his History of UFOS. Without the encouragement of all these kind people I would not have continued with it.

The book is part of my original Link to the Stars, which I hope some publisher will accept one day, and is for my grandchildren Tracey, Jayne, Gillian, Kerry-Ellen, Lindsey, Russell, Stephen, Amy and Jonathan.

Some of the illustrations and a few of the reports are by courtesy of the late Gordon Creighton, Editor of Flying Saucer Review

FOREWORD
by
Margaret-Ellen Fry

After writing my book Link to the Stars between 1995-1997 I wrote to Desmond Leslie in the South of France asking if he would write an Introduction to it. To my surprise and delight, he was most supportive. I had to parcel him the entire bulky manuscript. If I eventually find a Publisher for the book people will see his Introduction again, for recently I was advised that possibly my book had too many coloured photographs and illustrations, making it too expensive to produce.

I have accordingly taken this advice and divided the manuscript and this is how Who are they? has come about. My grateful thanks go to the people who had these strange, often very frightening and traumatising experiences and have let me write about them. Of course a good many researchers will not acknowledge that these abductions take place. For the numbers that I have written of here, there were many, many more over the years who came to Alan Hilton and myself for some help and understanding.

I am well aware that people take drugs these days and some may be having hallucinations. There were a few that I thought so, but people would not be reporting these abductions from all over the world, all with similar threads running through all of them, if they were not founded on facts. A very disturbing fact it is too. For what is the Aliens agenda? Nobody on Earth knows, yet we have to acknowledge the disconcerting fact that Governments and people in power are just as powerless to stop them as the people who become victims to them. Their technology is so many millennia ahead of Earth, that it seems like magic. Let us hope they are equally ahead of us in spiritual development.

INTRODUCTION BY DESMOND LESLIE
CO-AUTHOR OF FLYING SAUCERS HAVE LANDED

Did you know that the UK had its own Roswell? A giant orange UFO crash-landed near Bala Lake in Wales, and bodies, like those from the Roswell crash of 1947, were taken by the military, under an immense cloud of security, to Porton Down, the top-secret research station. What makes this episode so bizarre is that the military seemed to know about it three days in advance and were ready and waiting.

This and many other British UFO secrets are revealed for the first time in this fascinating book by Margaret Fry, making me wonder whether our planet may be a zoo combined with a botanical garden, for trying out new species – ourselves included. From time to time our originators may come back to see how we're getting on, to slap our wrists, confiscate dangerous toys, and to make certain biological adjustments. These adjustments have been mistakenly called evolution.

Margaret's story began on Sunday July 17 1955, when she was sitting in her car, minding her business, driving down Chessington Avenue, in a nice, safe-sounding place called Bexley Heath. Suddenly a bluish-grey, bell-shaped UFO plumped down in front of her blocking the way. The UFO remained silent and motionless for five minutes, during which Margaret and a Dr Thukarta, and some children playing in the street, stood around it gaping, and wondering what on earth this thing could be. It was round, metallic, had a dome, discernable panels, and three "wheels" underneath, similar to the UFO seen by George Adamski; someone she'd never heard of at the time. But whatever would induce a UFO to land in Chessington Avenue in Bexley Heath, on a quiet Sunday morning when everything was closed?

That UFOs are seen only in America is a popular myth. Not at all. They seem to relish East London and East Anglia where the most ordinary towns and plainest of suburbs have been awash with space craft of every shape and size, ranging from the vast, circular flying saucer, which covered two whole football pitches when it landed in Plumpstead public park, causing consternation among park goers, to a most incredible display of gigantic luminous "jellyfish" which went to town in an aerial display that would make the Red Arrows envious. Not only did the objects constantly change shape, but also a couple of large black motherships came and joined the fun.

Why should UFOs put on such a show for us? Perhaps it wasn't for us at all. Perhaps those in charge had decided to brighten a dull stint on Earth by holding a fancy dress contest for "The Most Original Flying Object"? Everyone joined in - Flying cubes, blobs, cylinders, fiery balls, giant disks, wobblies, you name it. Originality was the name of the game. No two UFOs were alike. Alternatively, such ostentatious displays

iii

could indicate that most UFOs are 'bespoke', 'hand-crafted', 'made to order'; individually designed to the whim of the owner. Certainly Margaret Fry has seen more than her fair share of originals.

Since her first contact with a landed UFO, in the middle of a respectable suburban avenue, on a perfectly peaceful Sunday morning, she has had over forty sightings, inspiring her to research many little, or previously unknown cases, which make up much of her fascinating book. As I discovered, after meeting George Adamski in 1953, UFOs appear to mark or tag certain people for observation; as we tag wild animals. Mrs Fry seems to have been "tagged" as an observer to observe them back! "Taggees" spend much of their lives enjoying UFO sightings, or space-trips, and sometimes not enjoying being abducted for scientific examination. On the credit side, UFOs have been known to give healing. Margaret Fry describes such an instance. In 1987 space people attended an operation being performed on a Mr R Jones of Penywaun, Aberdare, for his numerous maladies. To the terror of the nurses and theatre staff, the space people floated his astral body up to the ceiling, where it remained plainly visible to the theatre staff and medical students, while the space visitors obligingly did the surgeon's job for him. Most excellently, I gather.

Like Victorian naturalists, ufonauts are avid collectors. This book tells us how the crews of landed craft have been seen to collect such variabilia as a rabbit, a weasel, a wooden log, even a dandelion; and once, on 16 July 1978, an old car abandoned on a roadside, which they beamed aboard their mothership. Doubtless it is now in some galactic museum of early transport to amuse the children.

They also collect US. (Well, some do.) And having performed their scary scientific experiments, return us to earth unharmed. Well not quite. Even though the testers attempt to erase these experiences from our minds the long-term effects can be very unpleasant, even after hypnosis has restored complete memory of the abduction. But as we perform far worse, far crueler, experiments on laboratory animals, I don't think we should complain too much.

Not content with poking and probing, and just plain "showing off", (mainly over East Anglia and Kent) UFOs don't always leave a place quite the way they found it. A Mrs Sage, living near Chatham, had her neighbour's garden rearranged by a couple of men in a strange craft, who exchanged pleasantries with her before flying silently away. After their departure she discovered that some of the concrete steps behind her house and her neighbours had changed size, a brick shed had been moved bodily to the end of the garden, and the garden gate and a fine old tree had vanished. But her neighbour's burned and scraggy old grass had been replaced by a well-groomed "instant" lawn and

iv

a well-trimmed "instant" privet hedge. Best of all her new lawn had a great "instant" mature tree growing in the middle of it.

Another irritating habit is the way that UFOs change shape, or appear to, especially over eastern England. This can be simulated if you put a saucepan lid on the bottom of a clear pool and agitate the water. The lid not only will change shape but, if the water is sufficiently disturbed, will appear as several separate objects of irregular size and shape. These changes are caused by refraction of the water. Refraction of disturbed air surrounding UFOs could offer a simple explanation. Certainly Mrs Fry has experienced many such examples, her Blackpool Pier jellyfish being the best.

Some of her most interesting experiences took place after she's moved to Wales, where she interviewed a number of contactees and abductees, while her dutiful husband sat waiting patiently in the car. I would not dream of spoiling your enjoyment even by hinting of these. They are too fascinating. But I must mention our same Mr R Jones of Penywaun, who witnessed two UFOs and a large mother ship being sucked into the vortex of a "black hole" where they, and the hole, vanished. This, I think, is the first and only time that anyone has witnessed a "black hole" in action.

Since flying saucers burst upon us fifty years ago there have been many books; mostly rehashing, or downright plagiarising, earlier works. Mrs Fry's book is not only highly-detailed and lavishly illustrated, it has also a welcome quality of freshness and, better still, something new to say. I couldn't put it down.

Desmond Leslie
S of France 1997

Author's Note:

This was Desmond Leslie's Introduction for my entire book, Link to the Stars. Sadly he died before he was able to write a further Introduction for Who are they? once I divided the original manuscript.

CHAPTER 1

WHO ARE THEY?

I was sharing a house in Bexleyheath, Kent with my sister and small children in the 1950s. It is a dormitory town to London and most people commute to work there. The streets are tree lined and wide, but rather boring as almost every house is of the same design.

On Sunday the 17th July 1955 there was a heat wave on, it had lasted a week temperatures were well over 100°F. On Saturday, the previous day my three little children had been playing all day in the garden, by nightfall the eldest had a temperature. In the morning I went to the public phone box down the road, to call our doctor; few people owned telephones then. My GP was on holiday, but his relief a young Indian doctor came. He was young, a tall thin Indian. He did not tell me his name, I only discovered it ten years later through my own doctor. He was Dr. Thukarta. He examined my eldest and said we should go to the surgery immediately to get him medication, as he had a high temperature and sunstroke.

I arranged with my sister to care for the children whilst I took my second son Steve with us, as he used to be rather naughty. He sat in the back of the Doctor's brand new baby Austin car, and we set off. The road I lived on Hythe Avenue was about half a mile in length and from the onset the car was spluttering and stopping. After a while we became aware of a heavy shadow over the car. The rest of the sky was bright blue and cloudless, the sun blazing to the left of us. We kept peering through the windscreen, wondering what was causing the shadow engulfing the car. Eventually I asked the Doctor if we could stop "No fears, I'm no mechanic" he said

We then had to turn to the right into Chessington Avenue, and amazingly this shadow turned at right angles with us. By now we definitely knew something was above the car. It then finally spluttered and stopped. I then said, "Can we get out now?" My son tried to get out, but the doctor insisted on his staying seated at the back. Once out of the car, we looked up and were horrified to see a concentrated mass of grey cloud-like material just barely 18 ft. above our heads. As we watched this oval mass started spinning. It then slowly solidified, and we saw three ball-bearing-like wheels come down from what I thought was a smooth underside. My son viewing it from a different angle years later told me he could see a central cone. I did think it was landing and would squash us, but we were so shocked we did not think to move away from under it. However, the wheels retracted, and it continued to spin and hum like a top, combined

1

with a slight swooshing sound like the sea. There was absolutely no down draught, as would be under a helicopter. It then flipped up on its side, then righted back again, then flopped down at the crossroads ahead of us. We exclaimed, "My God, it's one of those flying saucer things!"

In 1955 few working class people had cars, so road traffic on a Sunday in a suburb was nil. The few cars that people had were parked on the road, and there were children playing hop-scotch on the pavement. I yelled out to them and they all came and stood around the craft with their mouths open. I then realised it was in fact a few feet, maybe four or five, off the ground, maybe it had risen. It seemed huge although when we measured the spot years later we found it must have been just under 35 feet in diameter. It was a typical bell shaped craft, although grey/silver/blue, it was not quite any of these hues, it was more like pewter than shining, in fact it looked just out of this world! We all instinctively knew it was, we were quite aghast, Steve had his face pressed to the window watching. The craft had indents or mouldings, that I thought must be portholes around the centre, below this was a wide ledge, and above was a rounded dome which had further mouldings for a door? What impressed itself in my memory was that the lower circular part was in sections or so it seemed with distinct seams and what appeared to be rivets. I do recall every small detail of this, so does my son. Although I related every detail in a letter to my aunt the next day and wrote notes and sketches into a Diary one year later on the 17th July 1956 I always refer back to these.

After 5 to 6 minutes of being absolutely still near to the road, it then tilted towards us slightly and in that position went up, making a swooshing sound. It wobbled from side to side, then stood still when a porthole opened up at about 100 ft. For the first time I felt real fear, thinking there had to be people in there, when it was near to the ground and we were standing at arms length from it, we were so utterly amazed at the craft itself, that we did not think of aliens or anyone being in it.

Once the craft was up at about 30,000 ft or more, we got into the Doctor's car still dazed, all the way to the Surgery the doctor kept repeating he did not believe in flying saucers, we did not even notice the car was running perfectly. After getting the medication, the doctor dropped us off at my house. Some years later when I decided to investigate this our own astonishing sighting, my Doctor Lobo told me Dr. Thukarta had reported the incident to the British Medical Board. How much notice did they take I wonder, they did not bother to interview me or those children. I have in fact tried to contact them over the years periodically without success as I no longer live in North Kent.

When we got home both Steve and I were excited in telling our family about the flying saucer, they reacted much the same as a cross section of people do today. My sister exclaimed, but said what use was that, why didn't they come out? My eldest son was aggrieved complaining he was feeling so ill and we were talking rubbish. My scientist father kindly informed me we had mistaken the sun. Only my Mother staunchly said, "If Margaret said it happened, it did". The following week she obtained the Kentish Times where there was an account of a policeman and other witnesses seeing a bell shaped craft low to the ground at Erith just after midday on Sunday the 17th July, 1955. She then set about finding a book about flying saucers. She found Flying Saucers have Landed by Desmond Leslie and George Adamski and put it by as a birthday treat for me. It never occurred to me to contact the newspapers or tell anyone other than my family, possibly because I knew we would be disbelieved. The only other person who at the time accepted that this happened was Martin Wilkins, the son of the late Harold T. Wilkins who was my sister's friend. Unfortunately Mr. Wilkins had just died that year shortly before I met Martin, otherwise no doubt he would have featured it in one of his books, and it would be more widely known today. Martin very kindly gave me some first editions of his father's books.

You might wonder how a person feels after having such an experience. For weeks I really felt I had my feet in two worlds, one with that craft that linked me to another planet. I also felt isolated, for my son was too young to discuss it in depth with. Gradually you put it out of your mind and get on with life, but you are never the same again. That was the start of my life long interest and research into the UFO phenomenon. Nine years later I heard of BUFORA and joined them at the end of 1964/65. I then met the Earl of Clancarty and he asked me to investigate for his newly formed Contact International. So I was one of the founder members of Contact International UK based at Oxford. I continue to represent them today. About October 1993 Gary Rowe of Rhyl and I decided to form the Welsh Federation of Independent Ufologists. This is more a fellowship that extends to the whole of Wales than an organisation or local group. People who are interested can join and take on the umbrella national name which is useful for dealing with the Press, T.V and Radio, but we all operate independently, whilst keeping in touch and liaising occasionally.

I continued to see UFOs from time to time and investigated other people's sightings in earnest. WFIU members and I still do.

Now I would like to relate in full, two of the three most important UFO events in my life. On the 26th July 1978 a Wednesday I was gardening, so was my neighbour Violet Lawrence, just the other side of the 3ft chicken wire fencing. We were chatting when we noticed a peculiar angry red area in the sky, with thick black streamers of cloud emitting from it. We assumed a storm was brewing, so rushed indoors, only to notice the sky outside in the front looked a serene blue. I sat down to watch TV when I saw a silver flash, and got up to draw the curtains. I am afraid of storms, but this was no

3

lightening flash, it was a splosh of silver slowing flying in the clear blue sky towards the houses opposite. As I watched it split into two, one half elongating and flew off in the direction of Barnehurst, the other coming to rest just above the house opposite me.

I grabbed my binoculars and rushed outside. I watched this blob slowly turn into a giant cobweb of lights, thousands of twinkling little silver lights directly opposite me, on what looked like an open umbrella frame. As I looked through the binoculars this lazily turned over, then upside down, then sideways, expanding, then going small, then enlarging again.

In absolute wonder I thought 'no one is ever going to believe this', so I virtually leapt over my neighbour's low fence and banged frantically on their door. After agonisingly slow moments they opened up, about to protest, when they were transfixed by this fantastically beautiful thing "was that what a UFO looked like?" "That is what this one looks like" I said. It could be likened to a giant spider's cobweb caught in sunlight after rain glinting in the sky. It was now 9.05 p.m. and being July as light as daylight.

Shortly afterwards our Football Pools Distributer and her father called at my house. I called to Deborah De Negri to join us. She ran to fetch her father from their car, and they joined us on the pavement, where we were by now, for this Cobweb had tumbled, twisted and turned over the house roof tops to settle about 800ft above The Green opposite. This was a play area for children in our built-up suburb of Bexleyheath, North Kent. There were children playing on this Green and they ran off to fetch their parents.

Now this silver Object set up a bemusing display. It seemed solely for our benefit for one hour and twenty-six eternal minutes. It twisted, turned upside down, enlarged and diminished. Periodically a small silver ball would appear, then a black toy submarine, these would swim about lazily in the cobweb. In fact the whole Object reminded me of the Sea anemones one saw floating about under the Sea in the Jacque Cousteau TV programmes. Deborah likened it to a cell floating in liquid, when watching things under Slides in her biology class.

In fact this whole experience gave me ideas I had never thought of before in connection with UFOS. Unless in direct eye alignment with the thing, we all saw something slightly differently, but if you took up the position of the person with the binoculars we saw it identically. There was also the puzzle of these Objects being able to diminish to the size of toys, then expand, at least so it seemed to human eyes. But then the spectrum of our vision is limited, this may have something to do with this. It was only occasionally, for example when it turned to a shape like a Chinese lantern, that we realised it was probably two black cigars making a display of light patterns for us.

When we said 'we wished it would come down, so that we could see what it really was', it seemed able to monitor our voices, for it would encase us in a beam of light, when we all felt it was teasing 'not this time, maybe next! 'People on that very busy main thoroughfare DID stop to ask what we were watching, and when we said 'UFOS' they parked their cars at the side of the road and joined us. The amazing thing was, none stayed long, maybe because we selfishly refused to share the two binoculars we were passing to each other. There were five of us there, Mr and Mrs Lawrence, Mr and Miss de Negri and myself. The silver cobweb was distinctly visible to the eyes, but there was obviously far more detail when viewed through binoculars. We were so completely engrossed, we never thought to ask these people what they were seeing.

The sky had gradually darkened when a small passenger plane passed over at about 1,800 ft. This Object was more than half way to ground level from it. Then very slowly a long black cylinder came from Woolwich side and gradually positioned over it. The Sphere stopped twisting and turning, and absolutely amazingly that whole area of sky turned as light as day. I could see a knot of people standing and watching the other side of the Green quite clearly, as these two out-of-this-world Objects went away in that position, barely perceptibly moving, until they were over to Danson Park area and lost to view, when the sky immediately turned velvet dark again.

As everyone stood talking, other neighbours had joined us, too late to see anything. It was now 10.30 pm. as I went indoors and phoned Maureen Hall my BUFORA colleague; she lived in Dartford and could see nothing. Our phone call was interrupted by voices that seemed excited and at a party. They seemed to come tumbling down from the ether, until we heard one metallic voice above the others. In annoyance we put down the phone thinking it was the MOD playing games with us, and tampering with my phone again. Then realising the significance of this, we rang each other again only to get the engaged sound, until we got through to each other and both exclaimed 'Asta Gallactic Command'. On the 27th January 1978 we had been invited over to Barking, by the Essex UFO Group to listen to a 'Space Message' in a tape sent to them, this recording was the exact metallic voice we now heard over the phone! Then I had to leave off as Mr. Cahill my Police contact was coming down my pathway. I went out to meet him, and so did my neighbours, all of us trying to tell him at once of this wonderful extraordinary experience.

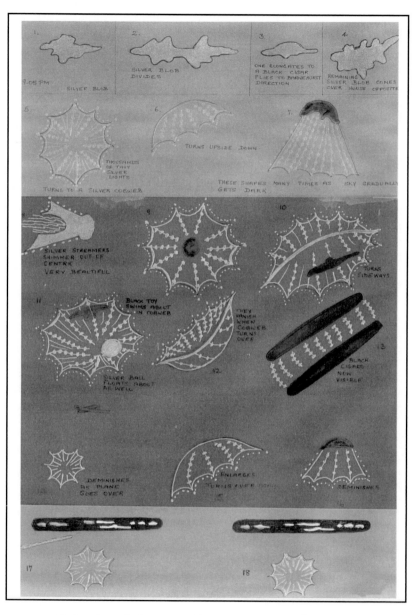

My drawings of what my neighbours and I saw on 26th July 1978

6

Mr. Cahill had peddled over on his bicycle from The Broadway, Bexleyheath Police Station to tell me that some teenage children had see UFOs that afternoon at 3.30 p.m. Sean and Sharon Kefford and their French pen-friend Nathalie Lefebyre from Paris on holiday with them had gone swimming, and were returning home, when they saw a strange cloud-like Object in the clear sky. An egg-shaped silver disc appeared and flew right into it. It then came out again and flew on across the sky, following the main King Harold's Way road line.

I went and interviewed these children on the 28th July. They were perfectly sensible and had the support of their parents. Mr. Kefford told me he frequently flew on business from Gatwick to Scotland and noted King Harold's Way was very prominent even at 14,000 ft. so he was not surprised this UFO had followed the line of this main road from the sky as the children told him.

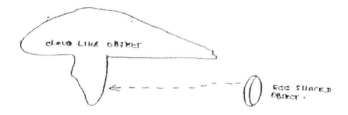

Objects seen same day, 26 July 1978 at 3.30pm, by Kefford children and Miss Nathalie Lefebyre of Paris, France flying down King Harolds Way, Erith, Kent.

A few days later Eileen and Douglas Clarke came over. On Wednesday the 26th July between 2 p.m. and 3 p.m. Eileen had been gardening in their small back yard at Barnehurst. Suddenly a helicopter swooped down from just over the roof of their terraced house, and hovered just over the clothesline. It came so low Eileen ducked down and fell over on the ground and in that position she looked up. The helicopter was brownish/black, had no markings and made no sound. There were two men sitting in it, one was looking down at her, the other looked straight ahead. They both wore what looked like knitted balaclavas, such as World War I pilots wore. They had quite ordinary faces. She got up and started to walk down the pathway. She completely forgot it and went indoors.

When Douglas returned from work, Eileen remembered it again and told him about this helicopter, and they should complain to the Air Force about them travelling so low. He said" surely the sound deafened you, and the rota blades must have blown you to bits". It was only then that Eileen realised there was something very strange about the whole incident, for she had heard no sound, felt no down draught, neither did the rotas blow anything about. The window was all in one and there were no landing gear, skids or wheels, and no markings at all. She normally noticed all aircraft, she was always looking at craft in the sky through binoculars, mainly because of Douglas's interest as a UFO Investigator. They decided to come over and discuss it with me.

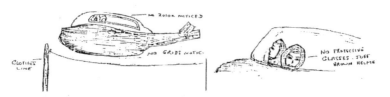

'Helicopter' seen by Eileen Clark on 26 July between 2pm-3pm whilst gardening

Pat Grant had given me a very similar report from Bearstead in Kent for the 25th July, 1975. A Mrs M Humphries had more of a football-shaped craft swoop down over her small terraced house, to just above her in the back garden, the Beings in it had transparent fish bowls on their heads. The whole of the circumstances were much the same.

Having received all these reports for the same day I was determined I would be open about this experience and tell the Head Manager at Woolwich Equitable, Bexleyheath, where I frequently worked in a temporary capacity. I wanted to put a Notice on the General board, asking anyone if they had also seen anything. The Managing Director who was in his 60's listened without interruption to me. Then he said quietly and with interest "Mrs Fry I note you wear a copper bracelet, is it effective, my wife gets considerable pain with arthritis." I just as quietly walked out of the room.

Numbers of the people working there, did come to tell me they had noticed the very unusual angry huge patch of red in the sky, which had emitted black columns of clouds, they had never seen anything like that before, and felt it was quite unnatural, as the rest of the sky had been clear blue.

A day or so after the incident I rang the De Negri family and asked if I could go over, explaining I was a UFO investigator and would like them to write individual accounts of what we saw. They were very pleased to see me, for they could think of nothing else. I showed them what I had drawn in water colours that night, and they said "perfect, we could not improve on your drawings". The Lawrences were the same, they never ceased to talk of their wonderful experience, and thanked me over and over again for calling them out. On the 26th July 1979 Mr. Lawrence was sitting out in the garden and said, 'To-day is the anniversary of what we saw, I will never forget it to my dying day'. At the time he was suffering from heart trouble and died shortly after.

I tried to help Violet through this sad time for her, and we only then became good friends, because at the time of the Sighting I had only been in the house three months and did not know any of my neighbours well. Violet now lives in Essex and could be contacted through me. When shifting to Wales I lost touch with the De Negris, but I believe Deborah is now a policewoman working in London.

The large Samways family who stood at the opposite side of The Green from us and watched this, left me wondering again that one has to be in direct eye alignment with this phenomenon to see it at all. When I went over in trepidation to the rough council Estate where this family lived on a road of people rather like the Battersby's of Coronation Street! I found they were more tractable than I had anticipated. Although I confess I did not hear what I would have liked to have heard. "The children had first seen a large and long black cigar shaped Object over the Green and had run in to collect their parents. They went out and this thing had stood not very high up over the Green for over an hour". Mrs Samways had gone back indoors once to phone me. I had reluctantly hurried in and out of the house to take the call, and stood by the windows to miss nothing. " When it left it passed directly over their heads, and the sky looked light", they said.

Had they not seen two Objects? Did they see the silver cobweb like sphere? No, they hadn't, they said. A short while after I met this woman with her eldest daughter at The Pantiles and again asked them if they were sure they saw nothing else. "That was all we saw", and they hurried away. I was puzzled by their behaviour, and wondered if her husband had told her not to talk to me.

On the 18th October, 1978 I received an unexpected phone call from a lady called Mrs. Mc Kinnon, 'would I come over to Barnehurst. She had been given my phone number by the Library, as her young son was pestering her, that he had seen a UFO with his friend Ian Diggen. He was a truthful little boy of 9 years, but she did not believe in such things'. I went over and the two boys were waiting for me with coloured crayons and paper. They were completely in earnest. They told how Ian was spending the night at Michael's house and they had been put to bed fairly early. They were playing 'monsters', and making shapes with the clouds, when they saw this black metallic craft without any wings, and white lines in it, come slowly over the garden. It was flashing, the time was 9.05 p.m. as they had looked at the clock, but did not want to call Mrs. Mckinnon as she would have said 'rubbish - go to sleep'. They also wrote down the date and drew what they saw there and then. It was the 26th July 1978.

They then very carefully drew for me again what they had seen, and painstakingly wrote out an account of their Sighting. I was astonished, for this was the craft I had seen elongate at 9.05 p.m. and fly off in the direction of Barnehurst. I told the Mother they were confirming my own sighting. She said "that's alright then, they can now forget about it and stop pestering me" ..... the reaction of some people is extraordinary. She clearly believed neither the boys nor me. At least she was open minded enough to call me, and let me interview the children without interruption.

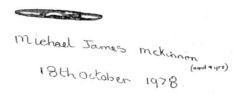

Michael James McKinnon
18th October 1978. (aged 9 yrs)

Object seen by Michael McKinnon and Ian Diggen on 26 July 1978

The only other references I have ever seen to Umbrella, or cobweb shapes in the sky, was an amusing and intriguing report in Week-end magazine August 1977, 'Farmer Jean Paul Gailleau was not shocked when his pretty daughter shouted that someone was flashing a light outside as she undressed.

This time he called the police then rushed out and grabbed two youths who clambered down from a tree opposite the girl's window. They said the light was nothing to do with them. It came from a strange Object in the sky above them.

When a police officer arrived at the farm at Saint Prochaire on France's Atlantic Coast, he said he had also seen the Object. IT WAS SHAPED LIKE AN UMBRELLA, he said and was spilling fire and changing colour from orange to green to red. The Neighbours who also saw it said it was making a strange whistling noise. The youths were allowed to go'.

Flying Saucer Review reported that on the 22nd July, 1978 a Doctor's wife Mrs. Catherine Dawson-Alexakas, her Greek mother and English father Mr. Dawson all saw from a car over a taverna at Chalandri, near Athens an Object. This changed shape to finally a dark cigar with "catherine wheels" of light around what appeared to be the front end. FSR Vol.25.No.1 1979.

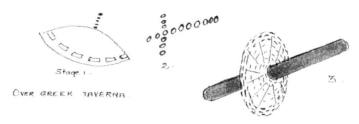

Stage 1.

OVER GREEK TAVERNA

3.

2.

The Object changed shape to finally a dark cigar with 'catherine wheels' of light

A further report in FSR Vol 26 No. 5 A lady called Aase Trautner was in a taxi passing over Fredericsbro - Fredrick's Bridge in Arhus, Denmark. Down below on the railway lines she saw a long,narrow dull silver coloured cigar shaped craft with pointed ends. This was the llth March 1975 at l.30 p.m. It was floating silently, slowly at tree top level above the lines. Around its middle there was a dense cluster of beams of light shooting out, as though rotating.... as the Object came to the Bridge it vanished.

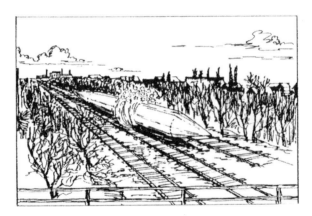

Our artist's impression of the scene by Fredericsbro in Arhus,
based on the FUFOS artist's reconstruction of the event

Taking these small reports into account, I felt that what we saw that 26th July evening was two if not three black cigar shaped objects giving us a display of lights.

The things we saw that year were really beyond belief, yet we did not imagine them, others always saw them with us. Any researcher sufficiently keen to check all this could do so with a bit of detective work in tracing all these people again. In fact I have to confess that as we saw these impossible UFOs so frequently in 1978, we got a bit blasé about the whole thing, and expected to see them - and we did time and again. I did not really appreciate how extraordinary these Sightings were until I was distanced from them by years, and noted that no matter how many new UFO books were printed, none related some of what I have in my books. These experiences were quite unique even in the annals of UFO folklore.

On 18th July, 1978 at 8.30 p.m. we were baby-sitting my four years old granddaughter Jayne. She was having a game of rough and tumble with Grandad when I suddenly spotted a fat bellied brown skeleton looking plane (see photo) dive down by the houses opposite. Jayne looked up, poised and said "Its one of your funny aeroplanes Granny". I insisted on us all going to The Green to see what it was and where it had landed. We went and there was absolutely nothing there.

About the 16th July evening at 5.45 p.m. I came out to wave Ron off to his night shift. I spotted a huge silent white dirigible pass slowly between the same houses opposite. It was a misty evening. I subsequently discovered this was the Goodyear Air Ship on its only trip that year to England, coming from Rome where it is based.

The 13th August, 1978 Sunday was a warm, but not too hot summer's day, no wind, with not a cloud in the light blue sky, so Ron and I decided to go strawberry picking. We went by car to Beesfield Farm, near Swanley; our route going through the village of Sutton-at-Hone on the country A 225 narrow road.

As we were coming to the crossroads by Eglantine Farm, a huge dull grey dirigible passed over our narrow country road just in front of the car. Ron was the first to see it, although he was driving, the sheer size of it distracted his attention. I have learnt over the years as a UFO investigator to be a pretty accurate judge of size of closer objects in the sky. This dirigible was at least 300-400ft long and about 40ft wide, at the widest part in the centre. I judged it to be about 700 ft above ground level, if that. It had distinct lines in it that formed squares, but no protrusions or lettering. When Ron shouted, "what the heck is that?" I looked up as it had just manoeuvred to alongside of us, just over the fields on the road leading to Horton Kirby. To the left of the car it was sailing along majestically and slowly on an even course. I shouted, "Why, it's an airship - how exciting". Ron slowed down to the same speed of the craft, about 10 mph so that we could take a good look. Then we came to some hillocks beside the road, so lost sight of it, as it was so low.

After this we turned on to the very busy main Kent motorway, the A20 where the landscape fell away to open ground, with a wide valley below the road. There were low hills in the background, wide sweeps of fields, and some densely forested areas further on. The dirigible was now ahead of us, still over this low-lying area. I noticed several hundreds of people gazing up at the craft from the fields about 200ft below us.

All these people had come to strawberry pick, and some were standing by their cars in the car parks of the Farms. The dirigible had by now slowly manoeuvred around over the fields, with its nose sharply tilted up. We were now approaching Eglantine Farm, as it stationed itself to the right of, slightly above what I now noticed for the first time. This was the weirdest Object I have ever seen in the sky. It was like nothing so much as a huge television aerial suspended bolt upright in the cloudless, windless, clear light blue sky! Below it, and attached to it, there was what looked like a huge limp, pear-shaped, light-grey balloon.

I had wound down the car window, and was leaning out trying to get a photo. I begged Ron to stop. "Impossible, not on a dual carriageway". He was going as slowly as he dared, glancing when he could at this spectacle. At this point the road was on high ground, and the fields well below 200 feet so that these objects were only a few hundred feet above us. Helicopters, all of them white, I noted, busily passed between the two Objects, this was the Gatwick/Heathrow Airport route. I wondered if the pilots could see these things, which were now absolutely still.

Then I looked higher in the sky, and there to my amazement were a whole fleet of dirigibles in some sort of formation high up spreading over the distant wooded areas to the horizon. They were as far as the eye could see, and all were stationary. I felt very excited thinking this must be some air display, as we were not far from Brands Hatch, the famous racecourse. I had not seen an Airship since before the outbreak of World War II when I was a small child in India. I concluded this must be something to do with the Goodyear Air Company.

We then turned off the main road, on to a farm dirt track, where I could still see the Objects, but once we turned on to Beesfield Farm to my intense disappointment we lost sight of them. I wanted to turn back, but Ron petulantly said "have we come strawberry picking or not?" So we got our baskets and went into the fields. All afternoon white helicopters busily flew over making a racket. I wanted to comment on all this, but the only people picking alongside me were Japanese tourists and Italians from the London Hotels. The helicopters had seemed like midges against these two huge Objects. I went on talking about them to Ron, until he agreed to leave early so that we could see them again. Needless to say there was nothing there on our return journey.

As soon as I got home I rang my son, after making sketches of what I had seen. Shaun reminded me Brands Hatch Circuit was not far from Charlton Farm, and it was probably an aerial platform for the BBC. So I just accepted these explanations, namely that the dirigibles were a Goodyear Air display, and the weird thing a BBC Air platform.

In February 1979 one evening I came home from work and switched on to 'TONIGHT' programme chaired by Frank Bough. He was interviewing a Mr. Anthony Smith about airships and balloons. I was amazed when Mr. Smith said he was hoping to build the largest airship in the U.K. At present Goodyear had the largest at 120 feet long.

As soon as Ron came home I asked him how long he thought the airship we saw on the 13th August 1978 had been, he said at least 400 ft. long. I now decided I would investigate this. First I wrote to Frank Bough, who sent me Mr. Anthony Smith's address, then on the 26th February 1979 I phoned Brands Hatch. A very helpful lady called Mrs. Webb replied that she was quite certain the Goodyear airship had not been in England on the 13 August 1978, and the BBC had not televised anything over Brands Hatch that day." In fact I know the Goodyear airship was only here one day, the 16th July 1978". I then recalled that I had also seen it at 5.45 p.m. on that evening, which she confirmed would be correct. Mrs. Webb suggested that I should contact the Goodyear Air Company and the BBC and she gave me the phone numbers.

I rang the Goodyear Co. and wrote to them on the 27th February 1979 and 27th March 1979. They were most responsive, sending me photos of their airships, dates of itinerary, and a pleasant letter from a Mr. Whitehouse saying I could not possibly have seen their airships on the 13th August.

On the 10th April 1979 I contacted the BBC Outside Organiser Mr. David Kenning, as Mrs. Webb had told me he had organised the Grand Prix at Brands Hatch Circuit in July, 1978. A Secretary replied and said Mr. Kenning was out. She had asked me a lot of questions, and said she found it very interesting. No doubt she told her boss all about it, for when I rang him I found him most uncooperative, in fact downright evasive. From the background sounds, he had on a tape-recorder, as there were clicking on and off sounds, and other off-putting noises. When I asked if the BBC was capable of putting up an enormous T.V. aerial that could stand bolt upright some 700ft in the air, with nothing attached to it but a limp pear shaped balloon. I was told "we do have air platforms.... then a hurried confused "something like that", and a slam down of the phone. This left me irritated, perplexed and wondering if the Ministry of Defence are hand in glove with the BBC in deceiving the public and covering up the subject of UFOS. For by now I knew these WERE UFOs, and how was it that a whole fleet of them could spread over the Garden of England, the fair county of Kent on a sunny afternoon, with hundreds of witnesses. Yet no authority official or otherwise will say or do anything.

I then tried to search for these other witnesses. In March 1979 I put an advertisement in the Kentish Times. I had no response, I should have tried a London paper, for I remembered most of those people had been Japanese, French, Italians etc.

In 1983 I had a break through, when at a BUFORA Meeting in Kensington, London, Bill Morgan and his brother came up to me and said they had read my article in Flying Saucer Review. They were amazed and delighted, for they were with some four friends, had been in a Group amongst the hundreds of people standing looking up by their cars at Eglantine Farm. What they were watching was the weird looking T.V. aerial with the limp pear shaped balloon attached to it. They were astonished because they had seen no dirigibles, how was that? .

I explained my theory about being in direct eye alignment. They had been a couple of hundred feet below us, when we were on the A20. Sometimes people just a few feet apart, one may see a UFO, and the other nothing. I recalled a case the Essex UFO Group investigated in Dagenham, where people on two adjoining Factory roofs were sitting enjoying a Lunch break, when all those on the one flat roof saw a UFO above and between the two factories. None of those on the other flat roof saw this.

In May 1981 I spent a few days in the high-rise flat of my cousin in Norwich. The poor fellow was dying of cancer, but insisted on driving my sister and myself to places of interest. He took us to Norwich Airfield to see the Goodyear Airship at its mooring mast. We also saw it slowly rising and flying past their block of flats. We went up to the 14th Floor to take photos of it.

The airship which was on one of its publicity tours taking people for rides, dipped up and down in the air. It had loud motors, and a distinctly visible cabin attached beneath the balloon, in which of course the engines are housed, and where people sit. We could see all this distinctly from the roof balcony. I judged it was flying about 1,000 ft up and subsequently got confirmation of this from the Airport. It had Goodyear written in huge letters on its side.

I phoned the Planning Department of Norwich Town Council to ask how tall the block of flats were, they said they were a standard 130ft. They were highly amused but helpful when I explained why I wanted to know! My dear cousin had gone to the trouble of helping me to do all this, for he knew I liked to thoroughly investigate not only other peoples reports, but also my own. Geoffrey Farren was one of my nicest and kindest of cousins. On returning home to Kent, I was so sad to learn he died three days later.

From all this I knew then definitely we had not seen any man-made airships on the 13th August, 1978 over Eglantine and Charlton Farms (incidentally the site of ancient Roman fortifications if you look them up on a Surveyors Map). The dirigible we saw was at least four times the size of the largest Goodyear air ship. It was also far more like the pre-war R 101 as it was ribbed and silvery grey, however it was much wider.

15

Mr. Anthony Smith had written to say I must have seen the Goodyear, as it came to Britain for two weeks a year, and was sometimes used as a flying platform for T.V cameras over Brands Hatch. Aerospace Industries had recently built an airship something like the Goodyear. This was undergoing tests at Cardington, Bedfordshire, where it was built. He added that neither air ship was over 200ft. long. As seen by the Goodyear's letter to me dated 27th March 1979, this expert's information was quite incorrect.

The Aerospace Developments Airship had been built in March 1979, so clearly was not what we saw. When Gordon Creighton decided to print my article in Flying Saucer Review. Volume 28 No. 4 1983 he troubled himself to ring Aerospace Developments Ltd., and found they had gone out of existence. They had been taken over by Airship Industries Ltd. He then phoned RAF Cardington and was told this airship had not been launched in either 1978 or 1979, it had only just been finished (1983) and was still undergoing tests, and was 150 ft. long. The BBC he was told, only had long shafted or long armed 'hoists' resembling the machines used in London and other large cities for servicing the maintenance of very high street lamps.

These were the most spectacular of my own Sightings. Over the years since 1955 I have seen UFOS about 46 times, every time they fill me with wonder and seem almost unbelievable, but then I remind myself I saw these always with other people, only twice when on my own. Then I have to take into account the equally fantastic and unbelievable reports I have investigated since 1965, often particularly in 1978 and 1982 with many witnesses, as far as I am concerned we are dealing with an Alien technology, believe me reader if you have seen these things as often as I have there can be no room for doubt.

SOUTHERN I. V. ALIEN BROADCAST by Dan J. Goring

On Saturday the 25th November, 1977 a remarkable 'space message' was superimposed over Southern Television News. The next day the News of the World contained a fair account of this very rare event- 'Thousands of TV viewers were stunned last night by a broadcast, claiming to be from another planet. The mysterious transmission came as Ivor Mills was reading the national news on Southern Television. It lasted about four minutes. Mills voice suddenly faded, and another man was heard warning that Beings from outer Space would take over unless the world pursued peaceful policies. The voice added "This is Gillon representative of Asta Gallactic Command speaking to you". Worried viewers jammed the telephone lines to Southern studios. ITN promptly flashed an apology on the screen saying the mysterious interruption was being investigated. A Southern Spokesman said later: "We've been flooded with calls. Our Engineers are trying to discover exactly what happened. We're assuming it was rather a sick hoax. We can't imagine how it was done, but it appears that someone must have managed to transmit a signal over ours. The equipment used would need to be fairly sophisticated and expensive".

LBC Radio had a 'phone-in' programme about the incident and David Basset who answered the calls said "It was obviously a hoax, as real alien spacemen don't exist!". Some people were convinced, though, that it was genuine, and the scene was one of disbelief and or bewilderment.

LBC were very fortunate in securing a full tape recording of the Space message — 5½ minutes - dropped into them by an anonymous person. This recording was played on a few occasions, but it certainly didn't sound like a TV-taped copy, but an original copy. A few people who were fortunate to have tape recorders at hand when the message came over the TV recorded various parts of it and played these over the radio, but they were poor reproductions for the TV message faded at times and there were background sounds from their rooms interfering. The LBC copy was perfect, however, and included not only the voice of the Spaceman, but the peculiar beginning and ending to the message as well. The initial sounds were an evenly spaced series of drumbeat-like noises, but with a curious metallic and reverberating tailing off to each beat. The ending lasted ½ minute or more, and sounded reminiscent of a West Indian steel band drumbeat! These latter beats were evenly spaced at first, but they gradually speeded up and finally merged into one long continuous tone. Very strange you will agree! If we assume the message is genuine, then it seems possible that these strange sounds have a psychological purpose to them. A number of abduction cases in the past have had a similar beginning and ending, such sounds possibly having a 'conditioning' effect upon the witnesses.

Anyway, I taped the initial part of the message itself and this was played back to our Group and the Kent Group who were invited over at Barking on the 27th January, 1978. The full Space Message was as follows -

This is the voice of Gi-lon (or Kilon) the representative of Asta Galactic Command speaking to you. For many years now you have seen us as lights in the skies. We speak to you now in peace and wisdom as we have done to your brothers and sisters all over this, your planet Earth. We come to warn you of the destiny of your race and your worlds so that you may communicate to your fellow beings the course you must take to avoid the disasters which threaten your worlds, and the Beings on the worlds around you. This is in order that you may share in the great awakening, as the planet passes into the New Age of Aquarius. The New Age can be a time of great peace and evolution for your race, but only if your rulers are made aware of the evil forces that can overshadow their judgments.

Be still now and listen, for your chance may not come again. For many years your scientists, governments and generals have not heeded our warnings; they have continued to experiment with the evil forces of what you call nuclear energy. Atomic bombs can destroy the earth, and the Beings of your sister worlds, in a moment. The wastes from atomic power stations will poison your planet for many thousands of your years to come. We, who have followed the path of evolution for far longer than you, have long since realised this that atomic energy is always directed against life. It has no peaceful application. Its use, and research into its use, must be ceased at once, or you risk destruction. All weapons of evil must be removed. The time of conflict is now past and the race of which you are a part may proceed to the highest planes of evolution if you show yourselves worthy to do this. You have but a short time to learn to live together in peace and goodwill. Small groups all over the planet are learning this, and exist to pass on the light of the dawning New Age to you all. You are free to accept or reject their teachings, but only those who learn to live in peace will pass to the higher realms of spiritual evolution.

Hear now the voice of Gi-lon, the representative of the Asta Galactic Command speaking to you. Be aware also that there are many false prophets and guides operating on your world. They will suck your energy from you - the energy you call money and will put it to evil ends giving you worthless dross in return. Your inner divine self protect you from this. You must learn to be sensitive to the voice within, that can tell you what is truth, and what is confusion, chaos and untruth. Learn to listen to the voice of truth which is within you, and you will lead yourselves on to the path of evolution.

This is the message to you our dear friends. We have watched you growing for many years as you too have watched our lights in the skies. You know now that we are here, and that there are more Beings on and around your earth than your scientists admit. We are deeply concerned about you and your path towards the light, and will do all we can to help you. Have no fears, seek only to know yourselves and live in harmony with the ways of your planet earth. We of the Asta Galactic Command thank you for your attention. We are now leaving the planes of your existence. May you be blessed by the supreme love and truth of the Cosmos".

Needless to say the press had a field day. The Sunday Express felt that a transmitter on some kind of link to land mines was used to get access to Rowridge and Hannington. The Sun said the Post Office had tracked down the hoax to Hannington, Hants. The Daily Mail said if the Post Office tracked down Gi-lon they would have him before Newbury magistrates. The Post Office investigators were working closely with technicians from Home Office Communications Branch. The IBA's monitoring unit, which keeps a constant check on the ultra high frequency channels used by commercial TV stations did not pick up a hoax. The Sunday Times decided 'it was students in a van using £80 worth of equipment run off a car battery'. Radio Jackie, a pirate radio station operating from Sussex, claimed they broadcast the message.

(Extracts from Earthlink, the sadly now defunct Essex UFO magazine by kind permission of Dan Goring the former Editor.)

There were endless permutations advanced for about a week, nobody was ever caught by the police, and nobody was ever taken to Court. It is significant that it was all allowed to die down pretty quickly by the authorities and newspapers alike.

It seems to the author of this book that the messages are too similar to ones given to Mediums and contactees. Would someone from some distant galaxy couch familiar sentences such as these? It is difficult to believe. I gathered that it would be very costly to break into a TV transmission with sophisticated expensive machinery. This point makes one pause to think, for who would have the money to do this, certainly not students, or those pockets of people who conform to New Age thinking. Who else would want to get such a message across at whatever cost? Despite my doubts, the clinching factor was that Maureen Hall and myself heard the same metallic voice over my telephone.

Dan Goring told me of a Lady he got to know quite well, the late Mrs. Jean Pilliager of Ilford, Essex. On the 27th May 1977 she was sitting in her bedroom with her dog at noon 12.30 p.m. watching TV when the picture went with a blind flash. When she turned the knobs 'foreign voices could be heard laughing, singing and music'. There was the sound of a plane, so she dashed outside; high above this plane, she could see two long cigar shaped UFOs the colour of unpolished silver.

On 12th December 1977 Mrs. Pilliager heard a recording of the Asta Gallactic Command message. Four to five hours later, just past 4 p.m. the phone rang. She was worried at the time as her daughter was having an operation. On picking up the receiver she heard the same noises on the line that are present at the beginning and end of the Space message tape. This quite terrified her.

In 1978 Mrs Pilliager received two crank letters on IBA officially headed notepaper. Dan saw these, and wondered where they had got her address, but she laughed it off. Again she received a phone call in late 1979 from someone who said he was from Capital Radio, London; the same weird noises were at the end of the phone call. He had said he would like to talk to her about her UFO experiences. Her phone was ex-directory.

On the 8th April 1983 Joan Pilliager died at her daughter's wedding reception. She had a blood clot just outside her heart.

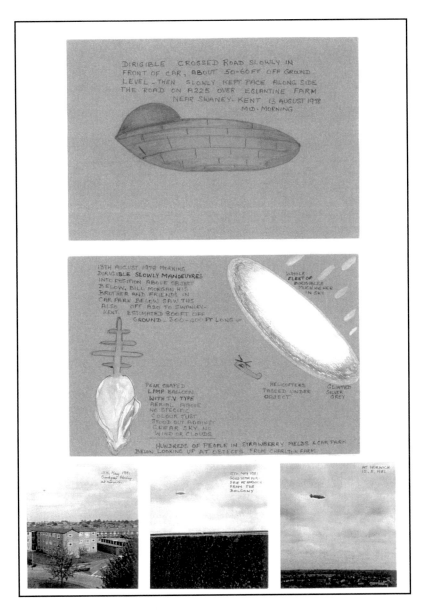

*Illustrations of dirigibles seen in August 1978 and photos of
the 'Goodyear' airship over Norwich on 15 May 1981*

THE SUNDAY EXPRESS January 7 1979

Up, up and away...

FIFTY YEARS before Orville Wright achieved the first powered flight in a heavier than air machine in 1903, a Frenchman had already tasted the delights of flying under power, in a steam-driven airship. Pictured here is a petrol-engined all-British design, the City of Cardiff, which in 1910 flew from Cardiff to London, a considerable feat for its 30h.p. motor. From FLIGHT WITH POWER, by David Wragg (Barrie & Jenkins, £6·95).

The R101—doomed to crash in flames across the Channel

CAUGHT momentarily by the camera between the Gothic spires of York Minster cathedral the airship 'Europa' floats gracefully on its journey across Britain.

Experts warned that Britain's airship was unsafe. But they were ignored—and 48 passengers perished

AFTER nearly half a century, airships are back in business. A British firm has produced a two-man, helium-filled craft with a top speed of 70mph and a range of 2,000 miles.

But whenever airships are in the news, there inevitably hangs the shadow of the R101 . . . the British airship that crashed in 1930 with the loss of 48 lives. Tragically, as revealed here, it need never have happened.

WEDNESDAY, DECEMBER 14, 1977

5.45 pm 16.7.1978

ENLARGED

This was the Goodyear airship

but what was the brown skeleton looking fat bellied plane? seen at 8.30 p.m. 18.7.1978.

Britain rules the sky with new mini airship

By JULIAN TAYLOR

A BRITISH airship—part of a multi-million pound export order—will carry television cameras filming the World Cup in South America.

A model of the Ariish Airship ordered by the Venezolanos.

Articles on Airships and drawing of 'fat bellied brown skeleton looking plane' seen 18 July 1978

THE GOODYEAR TYRE & RUBBER CO. (GREAT BRITAIN) LIMITED

WOLVERHAMPTON · ENGLAND · WV10 6DH · TELEPHONE: 22321 · CABLES: GOTYRUCO-WOLVERHAMPTON · TELEX: 338801

in reply please refer to MJW/321

27 March 1979

telephone ext 146

Mrs M E Fry
250 Long Lane
BEXLEYHEATH
Kent

Dear Mrs Fry

With apologies for the delay in answering your letter, I am attempting to answer the queries that it contained.

Whilst our company itself does, in fact, operate an airship around Europe, we only have it in this country for approximately one month each year - usually the period mid-June and mid-July. For the rest of the summer it tours the rest of the Continent and she is permanently based in Rome throughout the winter months.

With reference to your first paragraph, it was certainly, therefore, not our airship that could have been sighted in either August or September 1978 or in August 1970. Without knowing the exact date, I cannot confirm whether it could have been our airship over the Rochester town hall in the summer of 1976. For your information, that year the airship crossed the Channel to RAF Manston on June 17th and operated around that area the next day and then travelled up to Coventry on Monday, 21st June. From Coventry she operated at Southport, Sunderland and Doncaster before returning south to Biggin Hill in Kent on Wednesday, July 14th. She re-crossed the Channel to France at the end of that year's tour on Monday, July 19th.

In order to answer your more general questions about the airship, I am enclosing a press pack which I believe will give you all the information you require. I have also enclosed a copy of this year's itinerary.

Up until recently our airship, which in fact was constructed at Cardington in 1972, was the only airship to operate in the U.K. Another company, Aerospace Developments Ltd have, however, recently produced an airship a few weeks ago. This airship was also constructed at Cardington and the manufacturers can be contacted there. Your drawings are returned herewith.

Yours sincerely

M J Whitehouse/tb
Manager - PUBLIC RELATIONS DIVISION

Registered in England   Registration Number 223084   Registered Office Rushbury, Wolverhampton
ULTIMATE HOLDING COMPANY - THE GOODYEAR TIRE & RUBBER COMPANY, U.S.A.

Letter from Mr Whitehouse of Goodyear regarding sightings of 'airships'

23

Kentish Times

Comprising BECKENHAM JOURNAL, BEXLEYHEATH AND WELLING OBSERVER, BROMLEY TIMES, CHISLEHURST TIMES, DARTFORD AND SWANLEY CHRONICLE, ELTHAM TIMES, ERITH AND CRAYFORD OBSERVER, ORPINGTON TIMES and SIDCUP TIMES.

DARTFORD and SWANLEY CHRONICLE
(Dartford Post)
28, LOWFIELD STREET, DARTFORD, DA1 1HD
(Dartford 23004)
42, HIGH STREET, SWANLEY, BR8 8BQ
(Swanley 63283)

HOOLIGANS— WRITING IS ON WALL

GANGS of young thugs have be............... in an orgy of destruction through .... Road area. Families in Swanley are.......... towards nervous breakdowns. Villagers Hone, Hawley, Hartley and Southfleet........ destruction is making life hell on earth.

The most vigorous possible action....... restore sanity and discipline to this.........

We make no apologies for............ recent issues to the young thugs as .... An element of hooliganism or vand............. has always been with us and, short of a revolution in human nature, probably always will.

But when children, identified as being under 14 and in some cases only eight, take to using air guns, rocks and other missiles to intimidate the elderly, that is more than old-time hooliganism.

It is a mini-version of urban terrorism. Without the excuse of mistaken principles, the behaviour of Belfast, inspired only by the desire to frighten and destroy, has come to North-West Kent.

It is perhaps a symptom, and a controversial one among ratepayers, that Dartford Council are so defeated by the scrawlers of dirty words that they are considering putting up an official graffiti blackboard in the doubtful hope of protecting property.

Until recently, hooliganism was an occasional urban problem. Now, not only are there almost nightly stories of scuffles in Dartford town centre, but the once tranquil villages are becoming battle grounds. Rural bus-stops, bus shelters and garden trees are lucky to survive.

Residents are entitled to live free from nuisance at best, and at worst, grave danger.

For Kentish people, there is hope. The County Police have launched operation counterpunch. Plain clothes squads are on the prowl to catch the morons who think property is there as a target for their undefined frustrations.

Kent's plan is working. In one police division last month, there were 94 arrests.

The vandals had better think of changing their ways. At last, the writing seems to be on the wall for them.

OUR GAST... HERITAGE

WHAT'S COOKING? Some very interesting dishes — thanks to Kent County Council. Suddenly, KCC has become the housewives' friend, inspiring them to prepare new or rather rediscovered delights for their tables.

County Hall has gone into the publishing business— with a ye olde worlde cookery book. And to digress for moment, the attractive cover with its floral dash of spring is enough to fill you with county pride.

One of my pet theories has long been that while less illustrious counties make great song and dance about their native delicacies, Kent is coyly backward in coming forward to sing the praises of its gastronomic heritage.

Kent's position as the gate... food-minded Europe ... it unique is ... comes to ... for ...

.... en

In fact, my own inquiries in North-West Kent's villages a while back indicated most of the secrets, passed for a few preserved by W... stalwarts, have been forgotten.

Now KCC has put that right. A county archivist, Miss A. Revell, has delved into dusty old files of papers left by the 17th century county families and discovered their favourite dishes.

I would like to have seen a few additions. Such as Dartford's Christmas speciality, belly of pork. Or one or two items from Mrs Beeton, who had links with Greenhithe. But it is a mouthwatering book.

Consider Mrs Laybourne's rich almond cake, which requires two dozen eggs and three pounds of butter. Better ask for some more housekeeping money, madam.

Take 56lbs of beef!

But even that is overshadowed by another dish demanding 100 gallons of water, 56 pounds of beef and half a hundredweight of turnips. Somebody must have been feeding like 5,000.

"First catch, clean and skin the hare," one recipe begins. Another is for oyster sausages.

Thirsty? There are directions to make traditional Kentish brews, including Margate ale, which takes six months to brew before bottling. I imagine the hangover lasts another six months after that.

The difference between modern packaged ingredients and the original natural goods can make some

experiments hazardous. But Miss Revell says she has tried some of the recipes. And they are as good today as when they were standard diet.

The book is available, price £2, plus 20p postage, from the County Archivist, County Hall, Maidstone.

Airship – or UFO?

WAS it an air balloon? Was it a weather balloon? Or was it an unidentified flying object hovering in the sky over Charlton Farm, Swanley, last August?

UFO expert Mrs Margaret Fry, of Contact (UK), has written telling me of the time she saw what she first thought was the "Goodyear" airship on August 13.

But she later discovered that particular craft was not in the country at the time. So what was the object she saw over farmland where people were strawberry picking?

If any of those strawberry pickers can remember seeing the airborne object, I would be interested to hear from you.

Villiers link with N Kent

MR BOB DUNN, Conservative prospective Parliamentary candidate for Dartford, was as quick to answer my question as to whether the title, Viscount Villiers of Dartford, is still held by a living member of the family.

The answer is—"Yes." It is held by the 29-year-old eldest son of the Earl of Jersey, who lives on the holiday paradise isle, Mr Dunn is thinking of inviting him to visit the constituency.

The title was granted in 1691 to the staunchly Royalist family. They were given a subsidiary title of Baron Villiers of Hoo, which indicated they had strong links with North Kent.

For hard of hearing

AFTER our report on a proposed advice centre for the hard of hearing locally, it has been pointed out that Dartford has a district club for the hard of hearing. And its social agenda is fast becoming a weekly highlight.

Club chairman Mr Arthur Warren says that the organisation, now boasting nearly 80 members, was formed back in 1962.

Members meet every Tuesday afternoon from 2 to 4 at Temple Hill Youth Centre. Especially popular with old-age pensioners, the club

Advert in the Kentish Times requesting information on 'airborne object'

22 February 1979

Dear Mrs Fry

Frank Bough passed me your letter as I was the person he was interviewing about airships and balloons.

I do not know what it was that you could have seen near Swanley. The largest balloon now flying in Britain contains 500,000 cu feet of air which makes it about 120 ft high and 70 ft wide. It is dark green and has the words "Gerard A Heineken" on it. The largest airship is either the Goodyear or the one recently built by Aerospace Industries but that is being tented in the vicinity of Cardington, Bedfordshire. However, neither of them is more than 200 ft long.

Without doubt the machine that was flying near the A20 was the Goodyear because it often serves as a platform for television film cameras flying over Brands Hatch. It does have Goodyear painted in large black letters on both sides but from certain angles these are hard to see as most of its advertising is done with thousands of light bulbs attached to these two sides. The Goodyear airship is normally based in Rome but visits this country for about 2 weeks a year.

I return your drawings as you may wish to show them to other people.

Yours sincerely

Anthony Smith

Letter from Anthony Smith regarding airship sighting

CHAPTER 2

FIRST HUMANOID CASES IN BRITAIN

Mrs. Cynthia Appleton[1] who lived at Fentham Road, Aston, Birmingham twice saw a Being, who said he came from another world, right inside the Dining Room of her house. The first occasion was on 7 January 1957. Accompanied by a whistling sound the Being materalised and demateralised. He said they came to collect titanium from the Ocean beds, of which they were running short. The word had to be explained to her by her husband as she had never heard it before. He also showed her a television-like screen of the Craft they came in. He called it 'Master Craft'. It was circular, with the top half transparent. Cynthia's baby, Janet was in a pram in the room, she had one tooth, and by the end of the week she had six! The Being stood on newspaper, which had been placed on the floor in front of the fire grate.

On the second occasion, the 18 November 1957, the Being appeared again accompanied by another, again in her Dining Room. Both wore close fitting garments with a raised collar or ruff, both had page boy hair styles, both were fair skinned and appeared to be very solid people, not etheric at all. Both now spoke English, whereas the first time on the 7 January the Alien had communicated by mental telepathy.

They told her they had come from Valn, this country being on the planet Venus. She asked why they had come to her and was told she was one of the few people whose brain was capable of receiving such communications.

Many people interviewed Cynthia Appleton, including Clergymen, the Earl of Clancarty and Gavin Gibbons the first Editor of Flying Saucer Review. All testified to her sincerity, and the belief that this did take place. Over the years I have written to all the Appletons in the Birmingham, Midlands directory. Surprisingly I had a good response, but I have never managed to find THE Cynthia Appleton, I would love to know how these extraordinary experiences affected her thinking and future life, if she ever saw anything again.

A very similar visitation/s took place in Bristol 1965 to a Mrs. B reported by a Mr. Gerald Lovell of St. George, Bristol.

On the 21st October 1954 two small boys were returning from school across fields, to their isolated rented farmhouse. This was in the middle of nowhere at Renton, Shrewsbury, Shropshire in England. There right across the roof of their house was an enormous 'Mexican hat'. They yelled out to their Mother "Mummy, Mummy, there is a flying saucer on our roof". "Nonsense" said Jessie Roestenburg "Come in" but on their insistence Jessie came out and went to the rear of the house, where they stood by an outside water pump. They looked up and just stood still. The bottom half of the craft rotated, whilst the top transparent part was still and they could see distinctly two beautiful men with shoulder length flaxen hair gazing down at them compassionately, said Jessie. They wore the most vivid blue tops, of a hue we do not get here on earth. After a few moments the craft moved and flew away to leave Jessie profoundly moved and changed in her outlook for the rest of her life. She did feel ill for many months after though.

I phoned or wrote to Jessie for years before spending a day in her company in 1996. Both she and her husband are gifted, generous people. I got on with them exceedingly well. He is a wonderful artist and I have urged him to try and draw what his family saw. At the time I saw them, Jessie was writing a book, which I hope gets published.

In 'Link to the Stars' Chapter 5 I relate how a whole Squadron of men, radio operators at Calne, Compton Bassett, Wiltshire saw a 'rugby football' for one hour in a clear blue sky that same afternoon.

During the late 1960s and '70s Flying Saucer Review reported case after case of humanoid appearances. None of these Beings appeared to want to kidnap us humans as the 'Greys' do today. Incidently though I have been investigating so many years, no one has ever reported being abducted by a Grey to me!

Randall Jones Pugh the retired veterinary surgeon and a BUFORA coordinator reported the peculiar little Beings the children of Broad Haven, Dyfed, West Wales[2] saw by their playing fields on a damp wet day on February 4th 1977 at 4.50 p.m. also many sightings by adults of frighteningly large humanoid creatures all of which he writes of in his book The Dyfed Enigma Faber and Faber London 1979.

Dan Goring my friend and Essex investigator was busy reporting and investigating a Humanoid who had appeared in Epping Forest in 19672.[2] Whilst Jenny Randles repeatedly wrote for Flying Saucer Review accounts of humanoids seen at Bignall End, Staffordshire 31 December 1976.[2] A figure in a silvery suit beside a spherical UFO at Higher Fold, Greater Manchester on the 11th May 1976. At Rainford,[2] near Liverpool, Merseyside a Being in what one would consider an all enveloping Space suit on the 2nd January 1978.

Perhaps the oldest report was from 1901.[2] The witness, now an elderly man, told her of an experience he vividly recalled from when he was ten years old. He had been playing on open ground at the back of his house, in warm sunny weather. On returning home he came across a funny looking oblong house, with a door and a small turret sitting on the grass verge. It was green blue, with a metallic sheen. Two very small entities about 3ft. tall emerged; they too were dressed in green blue close fitting uniforms. They looked normal, except for their small stature; they wore helmets with two wires sticking up on either side. One of these Beings waved his arms about to warn him not to get close. Then they returned to the 'hut', which then became surrounded by an electrical arc that glowed. With a loud whooshing noise the hut or oblong box streaked into the air and disappeared over rooftops. The last he saw was a pulsating light.

It was many years before the Witness was to hear of Flying Saucers and Space craft, and only then realised this was what he probably saw, he was certain he actually saw all this as a child. John Judge my colleague from Margate, picked up a most intriguing case of humanoids being seen in the city of Johannesburg, South Africa.[3] Two English sisters were living in a Flat during the War years there. On a warm night at 12.15 a.m. 1946, having gone to a cinema, they were returning home, when they decided to walk the dog before turning in. They let it off the lead to go to a waste ground behind a Hotel and shops, then they heard a loud thud, thinking an African had thrown something at the dog, they went on to this waste land, and it was then that they saw an Object hovering 50ft off the ground by Hotel Langum. The War had just ended, so they thought this was some new type of craft from then. It was a typical saucer shape, with a domed top, about 30ft in diameter and 15ft high. The lower rim was brownish and the top bright gold.

Then they noticed that the dog had returned, and was sitting subdued by their feet. At this an extraordinary thing happened. The top part of this craft descended down through the saucer part and hovered directly over the Hotel. Then the ball moved back again through the saucer and above it. Two figures then appeared below it on the saucer. As they were virtually feet from this craft they were able to see distinctly that they were men about 7ft tall, wearing a white uniform, with brown belts. They had their arms behind their backs. They had short wavy hair. Eventually the Object floated away out of view of the Hotel.

Vida Goldsworthy returned to Margate, Kent in 1950, whilst her sister Mrs. Naudwin married a South African and settled there. It was not till Vida read the Daily Express articles about Flying Saucers in 1978, that she realised the significance of their experience.

Recently I went to Machynlleth[2], the surrounding countryside seemed to me to be steeped in mysteries, it immediately brought to my mind a report Andy Collins gave us in 1975. On the 22nd July, a Tuesday, a young lad had a most weird experience there.

The family was on holiday in the region and Trevor decided to take a walk. Over the brow of the hill, less than 50ft from him, he saw a strange object. It had a circular base like a child's paddling pool, 40ft in diameter. Above and in this was a rounded transparent dome about 7ft to 8 ft high. Trevor hid behind a boulder. He could clearly see two forms looking like "massive pieces of jelly" irregular in shape and translucent white with doughnut like white discs inside them.

These forms were changing shape and eventually floated through an opening, so he ran as fast as his legs could take him, back to his father, to whom he incoherently said something, but then decided to return. When he arrived back the blobs had returned to the dome. At this point the whole object began to flash in the colours of the country side; green grass, brown soil, blue sky etc. and accelerated faster and faster, until it blended in with the landscape and disappeared.

Trevor then ran back to his father, getting him to return with him, he could hear a strange sound, as wind passed through the long grass, but neither saw anything further. Not surprisingly Trevor suffered for this scary experience. He lost his voice, and then three weeks later became blind in one eye, he complained of thumping noises in his head. After awhile he became totally blind, this lasted for a period, during which he was taken to a psychiatrist (why not an Eye hospital?) and when Andy Collins and other UFO investigators interviewed him in 1978, his eyes were still affected. I wonder if they kept in touch with him.

Contrast these frightening other World entities, if they were that, with a case that always intrigues me. This did not take place in Britain, indeed the other end of the world in Viamao, near Lagoa dos Patos, southern Brazil, in the province of Rio Grande do Sol.

Five witnesses on a plantation by the sea saw this, the owner of the Fazenda, his wife, son, daughter and Estate Manager. The incident lasted at least 20 minutes. A hat shaped craft descended to a few feet above the ground of their plantation by the Sea. A reddish light which penetrated through the chinks in the windows, lit up the interior of the house. They all went out on to the verandah then the Owner and his Manager walked towards the landing area.

Two humanoids over 6ft tall appeared, they had fair skins, and wore white overalls with a broad band at the waist. They had long shoulder length hair and surprisingly bare feet and hands! The first and only account I have ever read as such. They started to walk rigidly towards the house.

Three smaller Beings also of a white race then appeared wearing brown overalls, they also had long shoulder length hair, but their feet were shod in small boots. They walked quite rapidly roundabout and within the perimeter of the underside of the craft. The tall Beings continued to walk up the pathway between the fields. They returned to the Craft twice, and a third time they followed another route through the fields to a Gate, which they opened carefully and shut - how different was their world from ours? Not much it seemed by their behaviour. The Fazenda Owner and his Manager had walked to an elevation in the land, then feeling unnerved, they hid behind some palm trees. The wife and daughter were behind a partly closed front door; the young son had hidden under his bedclothes.

The five dogs normally very fierce and challenging, sat docile and quiet. All were able to see the Beings clearly, for the light from the Craft lit up the whole Plantation. The wife called to her husband in fright as the two tall Beings approached the house. At this they halted in their tracks. They repeatedly did this as she continued to call out. Then they seemed to change their minds, for they turned back. When they reached their Craft, all five entered it, and it rose vertically, with a rotary movement.

Next day the feet imprints were still there, as proof of these mild mannered visitors. The investigation of this case was carried out by the Rio Grande do Sol Group for the Investigation of Unidentified Aerial Objects, Brazil. An account of this was sent to Gordon Creighton in Portugese which he translated for Flying Saucer Review. [4]

My mind returns to this case every time I am told someone has had frightening painful abductions at the hands of extraterrestrials. Surely there are some benevolent Beings out there in the vast, vast non-ending Universe? The little detail of the two tall Beings being barefooted intrigues.

During the Spring of 1978 Jenny Randles and her friend Paul had received an invitation to attend the premier of Close Encounters of The Third Kind by Stephen Spielberg in London. We had arranged that she would come down to my house in Bexleyheath for the event.

The Sunday Express had been running a headlined series of UFO reports for days and had a response of literally thousands of people writing to them. When a newspaper decides to cut a story line they do, no matter what sensational revelations come as a result thereafter. So they magnanimously offered these shoals of letters to BUFORA.

After the razzmatazz of the First night at the Odeon Cinema in London, the line up of famous faces and presentations Jenny and Paul were left to stagger on to the suburban train at Charing Cross, loaded with boxes and boxes of letters. We put them in bundles across my entire 32 feet long Living Room floor. As we tried to get them into some semblance of order by counties, here and there one caught the eye.

There was a letter from a Dr. Thukarta and family in Middlesex, but Jenny said "leave it, it will go to the Middlesex R.I anyway", before I had the chance to read it. I wondered if they were related to the Dr. Thukarta who saw the landed UFO with me on the 17th July 1955. I was feeling disappointed I could not at least take the address, when my eye caught a letter from Dover, Kent my area of investigations. I read it through a few times. This was the very first humanoid case I encountered, so I have never forgotten every word of that letter. I wanted to go down to Dover right away, but Jenny insisted that as she was Director of Investigations she had to list and distribute methodically, before sending them on to the R.I.'s (Regional investigators).

When I finally got my bundle of Kent letters, to my intense disappointment and regret ever since, this particular letter was not amongst them. I wrote to Jenny immediately, she did try to locate it, but then assumed she must have sent it on to Squadron Leader Alastair Provost. By then Alastair was dead, and if he had been well enough to interview this couple, which I doubt, his meticulous report, if he made one, must have gone on his wife's bon fire the day following his death. A great pity, I have regretted it ever since.

The letter had been from a middle-aged or elderly brother and sister who had lived during the War years in a large house by Dover beach. Depending on how old they were at the time; perhaps they were at school or College for otherwise the boy would have been conscripted into the Armed Forces. However, they did not say. It was an intensely foggy night in 1943 or 1945. Dover gets these pea soupers of fogs, so they had left the lights on, and taken down the curtaining, feeling the fog was blanket enough for the wartime blackout restrictions. The house was right by the beach, and they were decorating an upstairs bedroom for their parents.

As they were busy wallpapering, they just suddenly saw inches from the large bay windows a white craft hovering. It was like inverted saucers, with a wide band of bright blue separating the bottom solid white, from a transparent top. In this were two good looking young men, with long sandy hair to their shoulders. Dressed in white jump suits, with bright blue sashes at the waist, matching the craft. They were gazing with compassion at them. The craft was quite silent.

31

At this I immediately thought of Jessie Roestenburg's story. The brother and sister decided, "As they were foreign looking, whilst they were obviously male, they had feminine hair styles". This unheard of before the Beatle era ushered in long hair. "They had to be Russians," they decided "and perhaps they knew something more about the way the War was going, than we had been told".

Again it was not until the Sunday Express ran their UFO series the winter of 1978, that it penetrated this brother and sister what they had seen those years ago. It could not have possibly been Russians, so were they Aliens? Should anyone know of this in the Dover area, please do contact me.

NOTES:

1. Cynthia Appleton Operation Earth, Brinsley Le Poer Trench. Tandem London 1969, 1974

2. Flying Saucer Reviews
 Broad Haven School Report Vol. 23 No. 1/. 1977.
 Bignall End Staffs 31.12.1976
 Epping Forest. Vol. 23 No.1/ 1977
 Rainford Humanoid Vol.3 No. 6 and Daily Express 4.1.1978
 Machynlleth entities Vol. 24. No. 4/ 1979
 1901 Humanoid Vol. 24 No. 5

3. Johannesburg Humanoids in my personal files, but was reported in FSR Vol.
 24 No. 5

4. Rio Grande do Sol, Brazil humanoids FSR Supplement 5 June 1971

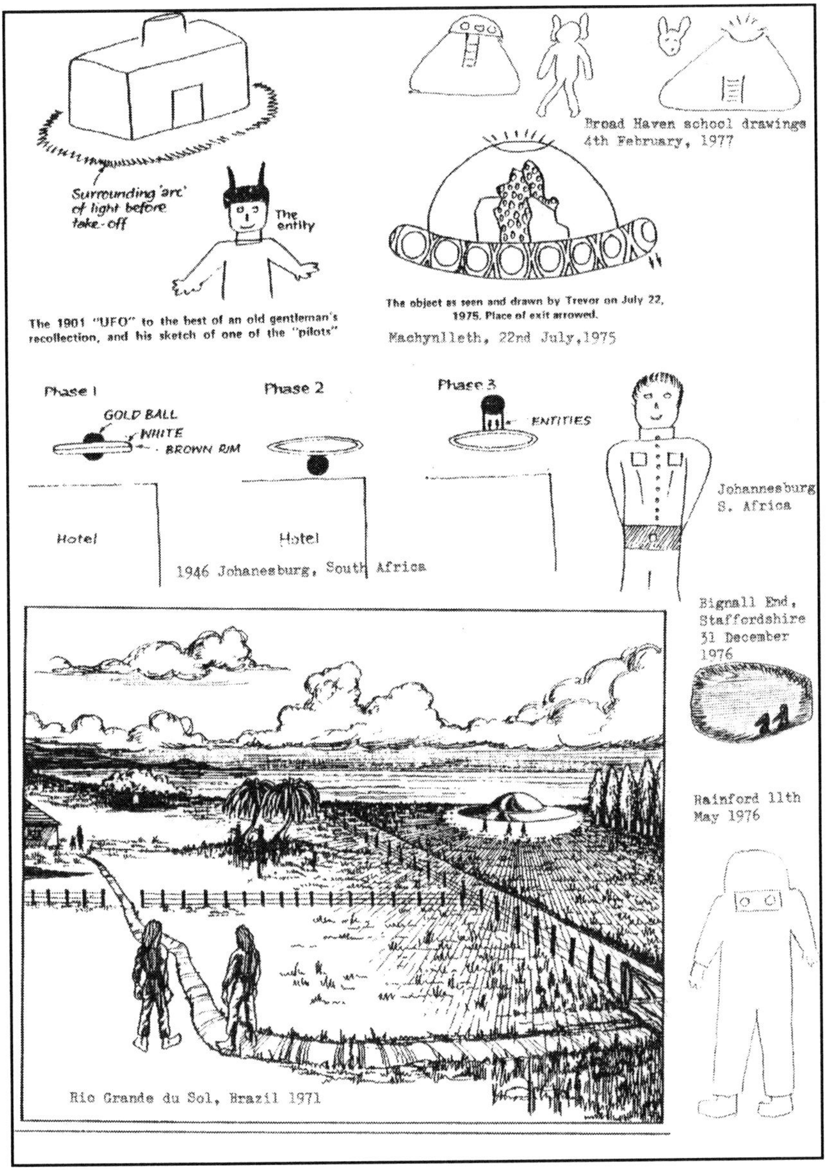
Surrounding 'arc' of light before take-off
The entity
The 1901 "UFO" to the best of an old gentleman's recollection, and his sketch of one of the "pilots"
Broad Haven school drawings
4th February, 1977
The object as seen and drawn by Trevor on July 22, 1975. Place of exit arrowed.
Machynlleth, 22nd July, 1975
Phase 1
GOLD BALL
WHITE
BROWN RIM
Phase 2
Phase 3
ENTITIES
Hotel
Hotel
1946 Johanesburg, South Africa
Johannesburg
S. Africa
Bignall End,
Staffordshire
31 December
1976
Rainford 11th
May 1976
Rio Grande du Sol, Brazil 1971

Sketches of first Humanoids taken from witnesses

CHAPTER 3

MISSING TIMES & ABDUCTIONS

Since the advent of the professional psychologist, and more sensible T.V programmes UFO abductions have taken on some prominence in the general public's mind. They do not probably believe this happens, but they are now aware of this phenomenon largely due firstly to Budd Hopkins[1] in the USA, a Sculptor and painter, he was the first to create a centre in New York devoting his time and understanding to UFO abductees - then the writer Whitley Strieber[2] achieved nothing but amusement and derision from the British media, never-the-less people were being made aware. Did he fare any better in America? There were others who quietly helped, such as Dr.Leo Sprinkle[3] Ph.D psychologist, late of Wyoming University, who holds private Workshop therapy for abduction victims.

In 1994 along came the highly professional professor of psychiatry at Harvard Medical School Professor John E. Mack with his book 'Abduction'[4]. The media could hardly ignore a man of his standing. We urgently need a few more men of this calibre to make the professions and general public sit up and realise that this isn't Star Trek, X files or some fantasy of Stephen Spielberg, this is for real. It happens to quite ordinary people all over the world, it is not just an American thing.

In 1994 Philip Mantle, then Director of BUFORA Investigations, one of our national UFO research organisations and Carl Nagaitis a freelance journalist[5] wrote a book called Without Consent in which it stated that in Britain a mere 40 cases have been reported. Reported to whom? BUFORA? Again, in a recent book by Jenny Randles - A Complete Book of Aliens & Abductions by Piatkus, seems to make the same assertion that she is writing about all the British UFO Abductions. Elsie Oakensen[6] was asked to promote the book on T.V. she enquired if her Abduction was featured in the book "No". "Then she hasn't written about every British abduction", said Elsie. The truth is, no author can claim to have a list of every abduction that has taken place in the British Isles. Our many small county Groups and also larger Associations are too fragmented and do not liaise sufficiently enough to make such a list possible, yet each of these endeavour to help individuals who come to them with missing time or abduction accounts. There are also private researchers, some very well known such as Timothy Good and others who work with these people, and what of the many, many people who do not know of UFO groups and struggle on their own to come to terms with this frightening experience?

In the mid 1970's, my friend Alan Hilton a professional physiotherapist/hypnotist and I teamed together to assist people who believed they had been abducted. We have not kept an account of these people, because they maybe talked to us the once, others wanted contact or help over a period of months, even years, all wanted us to keep their confidentiality. Certainly they numbered well over the 40 mark. Almost all the people written about here I helped over a period of time, they in turn have permitted me to write about them, often having the courage to use their names, for they want others who have not had the good fortune to discover people like us to know that help, if limited, exists.

In London the late Ken Phillips and Janice Georgiou established a Victim Support Group/Meetings[7] in January /February 1990 which Elsie Oakensen has very ably made known with her articles and books, then tucked away were the very small local groups and lone researchers who also started supporting and comforting people who went to them, such as my friend Joan Amos of Devon. Take into account that the same scene exists in many other countries, including the USA, I do not think their local groups are any more coordinated than ours and you get missing time and abduction figures going into many thousands all over the world

In a long conversation with Professor John E. Mack at Cardiff in August 1995, when we were both Speakers at a Conference, I discussed this with him, that it is far preferable to have a sympathetic ear, than nothing at all in the absence of professionally trained people. He whole-heartedly agreed with me. As to hypnosis, this subject makes the more sceptical researchers go ballistic. Having had two professional hypnotists Alan Hilton and Nick Garvey for our Welsh Federation of Ufologists fellowship, who have over 20 years of professional experience I think I hold a more balanced view. Not many abductees want to be hypnotised, I certainly would not, but if a person genuinely feels they can be helped in this way, I really do not see what the (more especially arm chair) researchers are kicking up a fuss about. It is surely up to the Abductee to decide what is individually best for him or her.

Hilary Evans the author/researcher wrote and talked about "the moral obligation to ensure that CE4 cases receive appropriate professional support" as he argues that Ufologists are not trained psychologists, psychiatrists. Of course, we are not, but in the absence of the mainstream of professional help, to date credited researchers have made a pretty sensible job of assisting people. In fact a professional psychologist/psychiatrist can do more harm than good if they cannot view this with an open mind, but I do in fact see the day of the amateur Ufologist coming to an end, as more and more people in professions at last wake up to the fact that the UFO phenomenon is worthy of study, we will be muscled out and considered of no consequence, that is human nature. This is what John E. Mack said to me "If the professionals do take over, some of them will do more harm than good, people like you should not underestimate yourselves as 'counsellors' I found him a very perceptive and unassuming man. He was right, the same point goes with UFO researchers, some are professional sceptics, they earn their reputations and living from this stance. I would advise any 'abductee' to be chary of whom they choose to confide in, a lot of these people can do them more harm than good It is distressing enough having this traumatic experience, without having to contend with someone disbelieving you, select someone with an open sympathetic mind.

Many researchers argue the actual validity of a physical UFO abduction. Having listened to and advised people from all walks of life for so many years, I really do think that *some* of these abductions are physical ones, but are these Beings on the same dimensional level as ourselves? Maybe certain species of Aliens might exist in our same three dimensional level, but are sufficiently advanced to use a fourth dimensional space time to confuse their poor human victims. Or is it just a question of a technology so much in advance of ours as to seem so? I have an open mind about all this, for having grown up in British India I accepted the idea that it was perfectly feasible for Holy Men (Sadus) to levitate, cause materialisations, have out-of-body experiences. Bhuddist monks, through years of meditation are able to enter a fourth dimension/or higher levels of consciousness. Generally speaking ordinary poor people are on a much higher spiritual level in India, than the materialistic Western world, particularly the Himalayan hill people, the Paharees, and they were my constant companions throughout my childhood.

Maybe because of my background I accept fourth dimensional Beings more readily than some fellow Ufologists. I do not though, accept that this phenomenon is the same as what we call the psychic world. Whether ghosts are spirits of the dead, who have gone over to another dimensional world living along side ours, or whether they are images or voices that go into the ether, and are picked up on momentary occasions by the human transmitter - our brains, who is to say at this present time in our too materialistic development.

I have seen ghosts on three separate occasions during my teenage years in India. In Wales I have seen ghost cats, a bright red brand new tractor on a narrow rural mountain lane, plus the following year on the same stretch of road a large brown car both of which vanished before the eyes of my husband and self as we swerved to avoid these vehicles. Then seen not only by ourselves, but all the villagers of our rural village - ghost planes, and lately I saw an elderly lady walk down the full length of my hall and vanish. On one memorable and frightening occasion after almost all the villagers bar my husband and self saw two UFOs land in farms on the 14th April 1984 night, in Llangernyw district, North Wales- that night a couple of Beings came through the wall of my bedroom and beckoned to me, petrified, I jumped on to my husband's bed and we clung together. We were not asleep and we did not mistake this phenomena for ghosts, instinctively you know it is quite different. It is my view that they are not one and the same phenomenon. Do 4th dimensional alien intelligences see our other dimensional dead, and are better able to communicate with them than us living three-dimensional creatures? Do they also see us only in flashes, or at particular alignments and areas? It is a thought and an intriguing one. Dr. Jacques Vallee the French astrophysicist wrote a number of books on his theories of multi-dimensional worlds peopled by non-bodied intelligences. Well, no doubt the billions of Universes are as diverse and far more weird than we can ever imagine, and at the present time we are just on the threshold of discovering the extraordinary diverse planets we have in our own Universe. At the moment NASA tell us they are uninhabited. But Hey Ho, if some of them are home for the Intelligences that Dr.Vallee and others have written of! There are some so called UFO experts who are so dogmatic about their UFO theories, they allow no room for the thoughts and study of others, they are the losers, for we are all stabbing in the dark on this subject and nobody is any more an expert than the next one.

All the people whose experiences I have given had totally different personalities, backgrounds and religious beliefs; some but by no means all had similar spiritual ideas and a few none at all. I felt they reacted to their experiences depending on which type of Alien Beings or Intelligences 'abducted' them. I was always reminded of Lord Dowding, whose views I wholeheartedly endorse. Our British Air Chief Marshal, Lord Dowding, was Commander-in-Chief of RAF fighter pilots during the last European War. He told the London Sunday Dispatch, "I am convinced that these objects (UFOs) do exist and that they are not manufactured by any nation on Earth....I think that we must resist the tendency to assume that they all come from the same planet, or that they are actuated by similar motives. It might be that the visitors from one planet wished to help us in our evolution from the basis of a higher level to which they had attained. Another planet might send an expedition to ascertain what have been those terrible explosions which they have observed, and to prevent us from discommoding other people besides ourselves by the new toys with which we are so light-heartedly playing. Other visitors might have come bent solely on scientific discovery and might regard us with the dispassionate aloofness which we might regard insects found beneath an upturned stone".

Before relating missing time or abduction cases I have personally been involved with, since forming the Welsh Federation of Ufologists in October 1993, I have noted more and more young people are interested in the subject, but few have been able to purchase old books and magazines about the Case Histories of UFOs. So for the benefit of them, the most famous abduction of all, the details were sent to me by my family in Moorrabin, Victoria, Australia, and later by Australian UFO pen-friends.

The Bass Straits between Victoria and Tasmania, over the years have yielded several mystery plane disappearances - the first being a military plane that vanished in July 1920, whilst looking for a missing schooner. On the 19th October 1934 a new four-engined mail plane carrying 10 passengers from Launceston to Melbourne vanished in a clear blue sky over the Bass Strait. On the 2nd October 1935 a plane left Melbourne for Tasmania and vanished at 9.51 a.m. On 22nd October 1978 a passenger plane with 9 people aboard vanished and 12 hours earlier Frederick Valentich aged 20 disappeared over the Bass Strait. In each of these cases strange lights and phenomena were seen in Victoria from the shores at the time.

Valentich vanished after reporting his DSJ Cessna was being dogged by a cigar-shaped UFO. The conversation between him and Flight Service Unit Moorrabin airfield lasted half an hour and continued to the very moment the pilot disappeared, he had been heading for King Island, and it was speculated that the Cessna was drawn into an enormous UFO, for although the Cessna carried 4 polystyrene life jackets, and its wings were designed to float, nothing was ever seen or recovered from the sea, although sophisticated well equipped RAF planes searched.

From 1st January 1978, this part of Australia had unprecedented UFO reports, many of these seen over the Bass Straits right up to the 20th October. In North Kent I too was getting an unprecedented number of UFO reports, in that one year I interviewed 246 people, and my weary husband seriously implored me to mentally communicate with them and tell them to go away! Nonetheless, on at least 7 occasions that year we actually saw these UFOs with the witnesses when called out by them. The Valentich case totally fascinated me. People continued to report UFOs over the Bass Straits into November. By the 21st December they were over the Clarence River area of New Zealand buzzing an Argosy freight plane. By the 30th December Quentin Fogarty a senior reporter and cameraman Dave Crockett over Cook Strait had videoed UFOs which made round-the-world TV viewing. Although these were picked up on radar in Christchurch and Wellington, seen by innumerable people from the shore and verified by seasoned pilots Bill Startup and Bob Guard, the theories Officials and sceptics advanced were so bizarre, as to make the alleged saucers themselves seem commonplace, said seasoned Ufologists from Australia and New Zealand, as it happened my cousin-in-law Harry Andrews was one of them.

Travis Walton and a group of foresters were woodcutting near the small village of Snowflake, Arizona, when on the 5th November 1975 a UFO appeared over the woods. Travis went forward to investigate, when a blue beam shot out and dropped him to the ground senseless, at this the other men bolted into their pick-up truck and beat a fast retreat, recriminating each other for abandoning Travis, they decided to return, but there was no Travis. They went to the Sheriffs Office and a search was instituted, but within days people were accusing the six men of murdering their companion. For five days they were harassed, until Travis reappeared on the highway into Heber very much the worse for his harrowing experience. He did recall some fragments of his abduction, but as with all these cases there were memory blanks. Timothy Good was able to visit this young man and hear first hand what he felt had happened. There is now a video based on Travis's story 'Fire In the Sky' VHR 2776 Paramount Pictures.

There was a similar case right from a suburb of Paris, Clergy-Pontoise. Three young men were loading their van at dawn, when they saw a large luminous cloud, Franck Fontaine 19 years, got in the van and chased after this when it turned to a saucer brightly lit and twirling, whilst the other two ran indoors to fetch a camera. On returning they found four bright lights surrounding the van, they then vanished and so had Franck! This occurred on the 20th November 1979. He reappeared on the 3rd December still wearing the blue jeans and red sweater he had disappeared in. When asked by his parents, wife and police where he had been, he was unable to account for any of the lost time. The police said if these three young men had been wasting their time, they would have them prosecuted, well they never were.

On the 23rd April 1979 a Chilean Army Corporal Armando Valdes was on a routine duty on the Bolivian border when he saw an intense bright light 500 metres from him. He went to investigate and disappeared. Fortunately for him he reappeared amidst his battalion unconscious, and with several days growth of beard!

Of course these types of alien kidnaps, with the hapless victims disappearing for days on end have never happened in our small British Islands. Think again!

Willie - Whispering Sands, Llŷn Peninsular

Willie's mother, a widow, had attended to the cow, and done all the necessary chores attendant upon an impoverished smallholding in North Wales in the Llŷn Peninsula. On this particular morning between 1886 to the 1890s, this lady had given a catalogue of household tasks she had already completed to her son, for it was the annual Fair day in Pwllheli. She was about to catch the big breaks[8] which came to collect people from outlying villages and hamlets for the fun of the Fair. "Now Willie bach" she said, "I have done all this, you get the Broc - Môr (drift wood) as much as you can, as we are baking tomorrow"

'Now you have nothing else to do, so go you to the beach, and the woods and collect a big bundle'. 'All right Mam, don't worry, I will' said the youth. So Willie walked down from their little wooden bungalow which is in the hamlet of Saron[9] above the Whistling Sands beach, whilst his Mother walked to the nearest village Aberdaron to board the breaks which was a type of fatan, horse and coach carriage. Willie had collected a huge bundle of driftwood and stacked it where the woods met the beach, when he heard a funny noise coming from the Whistling Sands; he walked down on the sands and a huge black thing landed near him. Two little men 'dressed like doctors' came out of a door in it and walked towards him. They were talking, but Willie could not understand a word that was said, 'they were not big men mind, but they forcibly carried Willie to the craft, and took him in'.

Willie's Mother returned from the Fair at 5p.m. and went into the house 'in them days mind, nobody shut their houses in Wales' (Author's note, and they still didn't until the middle of the 1980s) but no sound or sight of Willie bach. So she went down to the beach and found the huge bundle of drift wood neatly stacked at the edge of the woods, and just beyond a huge round circle, a depression, 'a hole, you know', at this the Mother thoroughly alarmed, walked to Aberdaron to fetch the village bobby (police man). She explained all the above, adding that Willie had not lit the fire, of prime importance in any 19th century home. So the Bobby returned with her to look all over, but by then the tide had come in and washed away the round holes. However, all the evidence pointed towards Willie having been drowned, but they would bide a while. Well, they did and after two weeks arrangements were being made for a Memorial Service for poor Willie, his Mother having resigned herself for the loss of him. A whole week after this she was cooking over the fire, when in walked Willie, "Well now, Willie bach where have you been? I was that upset, we looked everywhere"'. He looked different, his hair was long, he was in a trance and he looked rough. He said wearily "Look you Mam, I am very tired, I will tell you after I have had my naps", with that he sat down and fell asleep. It wasn't till the next day that he told his mother about the wonders he had seen. He described how 'they' had forcibly put him in their craft, and it had gone "strath up - not sideways, strath up and up" then they landed, he did not know where, but they took him immediately into a great big building, where they put him on a table and took something from him "they wouldn't have taken him there if they did not want something from him, would they? But everybody he saw there was smiling at Willie and they were more forward in everything; the colours of the place were amazing to him.

This story has been handed down in the family of Mrs. Edwards now living at Ruthin, but from the village of Aberdaron. She was an old lady of 87 years and she recalls her grandmother first telling her this story in 1914, so not so long after the event. She is a typical village North Walian, brought up in a rural area, so therefore having lead rather an insular life. She described how Willie had to put up with a lot of disbelief and ragging, until one evening when he was in a Pub, and they were at it again, in walked a man from Aberdaron, and hearing this yarn being repeated yet again, said 'hang on a minute, I was too far away to see the craft on Saron beach, but I did see it rise up from that area from Aberdaron and go straight up into the sky.' After this everyone said, it must have happened to Willie.

I must comment that as a UFO investigator I was fascinated, but frustrated by this interview. I had hoped to speak to Mrs. Edwards myself, my friend Margaret Hainge-Lloyd having conducted the initial interview had asked if she may tape it, she wanted a record of the old lady's memories of days gone by. Needless to say she was very happy to chat on about her own paranormal experiences etc. So such vital questions as, did Willie remember what happened after this 'examination' unfortunately we will never learn, due to the warring of Mrs. Edward's daughter and son. The daughter was under the impression that her brother had sent Margaret to 'spy on her' so she was told never to come again. As it happened this was totally untrue, but anyone listening to this tape, would realise it is an authentic and vivid recall of family history.

In the summer of 1995 I was told of a similar case of a lady being abducted and disappearing for three weeks in South Wales, to date I have been unable to follow this up.

The mind boggles at what would have happened had Willie been put through a well-known psychiatrist's hypnotic sessions, as Abductees are today! What would have happened to sleepy Saron in 3 tense weeks with the media hype of today? As it was this story never even got in the local newspapers of the day. Strange though that some hundred years later, another little Welsh village youth was abducted less than 7 miles from the same locality.

NOTE: Credit: Margaret Hainge-Lloyd

Youth Abduction - Llŷn Peninsular 8th February. 1985

During the night of the 8th February 1985, a 19-year-old village boy was walking home after spending an evening playing records and chatting with friends near Pwllheli. It was a long walk on the main road, the A499, of the Llŷn Peninsula. It is quite normal for our youngsters to walk 15 to 20 miles home in rural North Wales, as we have no public transport and taxis would be ruled out as too expensive. It is not unusual for a passing car or even a police car to offer a lift home at night, since most people are known to everybody.

The youth lived in a small hamlet further down the Peninsula, and had reached a point where there in a disused wartime RAF airfield[10] (three and a half miles from Pwllheli) The_____ was scattered snow on the ground, but this was a bright moonlit night and gla_____ to the field opposite, he _____ see an unusual _____raft on the ground, his curiosity aro_____ he decided to investigate, and _____ a na___row lane, leading to a farm on the _____ side. This ha____ckly bramble___ hawthorn hedges on either side of this mu___ track_____ into the ____ field where he stopped. He had bee____ hearing _____ is a piece of _____ land jutting out to form Carreg yr_____d not settled here, but the field wa_____ just past the gate _____ range black craft hovering just ab_____ 20 ft high, it had a glow. After wa_____ut by now there was a Being to the _____ propelled him towards the craft, wh_____way. As the gate is not clear of br_____if he was floated over the top. I rai_____v if he floated or walked, these rol_____helmeted, had stiff movements lik_____terrified him. He was propelled int_____sed into what seemed to be the Cr_____n on the wall. The Beings co_____eparing him for a Time change and decontamination. He then thought the craft took off, although again when we discussed this some years later, he said he could have been seeing what transpired on a 3D-like screen, for he passed or was shown the planets and satellites of our solar system, he quite accurately described some of these, which was what impressed me the most, no way could this boy have had access to the pictures NASA sent back by the Voyager probe. When they were past the planet Pluto they appeared to dock into a huge mother craft.

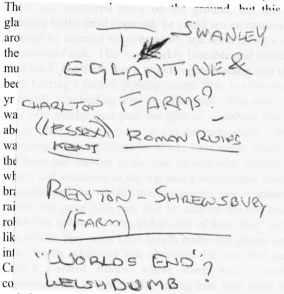

On this ship he was subjected to the usual type of medical examination which Abductees all over the world have had to endure. The youth had his left arm burnt by an instrument. This was later shown to Derek Mansell and my Contact International UK team. Most terrifyingly he had his heartbeat increased and decreased, at one stage they even tried to remove his eyes from the sockets, but he strenuously refused this; they seemed to be reading his thought waves. They informed him they came from the constellation of Lyra and had a base on this planet at Greenland. They told him they had captured a Voyager probe and found it to be primitive. They, in fact were quite informative with this youth, and unlike most abductees, did not have his memory obliterated. The Reader should not imagine this teenage man talked freely about all this at once. The ordeal was so terrifying and painful that for years after he would only let dribbles of these nightmare memories steep through his consciousness, sufficiently to let him talk about it in fragments. He was aware of being returned to earth many hours later, and vaguely recalled the craft leaving, he felt he had been away 6 hours. He was now several yards further up the A499 and still had a sensation of floating, as he walked unsteadily down the road in the early hours of the morning. A police car stopped and gave him a lift back to his hamlet at 5.30 a.m. where he lived in a large house in the centre, with his Grandfather, Mother and sister. There were up, anxious as to what had happened to him, he was shocked but gave them some fragments of what had occurred to him, he felt and looked so ill his mother went to Pwllheli Library to see if she could find a book on UFOs. Apparently she found one with the address of our former Chairman Fred Passey in it, and she managed to phone him. He contacted my Oxford Headquarters.

As the youth continued to feel ill, his Mother was very concerned and eventually on the 17th February she insisted on taking him down to Oxford, not feeling she could get help any way else. They left in thick ice and snow at 1.00a.m. driving through a snow storm and arriving at Wheatley in the early hours of the morning. Derek Mansell who'd worked a night shift, found them sitting in their car outside his house at 8.00 a.m. The mother explained, whilst the boy sat huddled and frightened in the car, he refused to get out and enter Derek's house. He then phoned a Colleague, and they tried to reassure him and got a disjointed account of what occurred. They promised to come to Wales as soon as the weather permitted.

It is normal practice to have the courtesy to inform the local UFO Investigator researcher and then perhaps join forces with the person to investigate these CE3 and CF4 cases, so I got a very apologetic phone call from Derek explaining that the boy had refused to meet anyone further. They were only able to get up to North Wales on a Sunday the 24th February 1985, 16 days after the event. The team consisted of Derek, our President Geoff Ambler and David Ridge. They went to the hamlet home of the Witness and met his family. The youth was calmer now, but still only talked of his experience in fragments. He showed his arm which still had faint burn marks. Nobody in his family disbelieved him, they are quite a normal village family, a large proportion of people are unemployed, but there are no drugs, etc. problems here thank goodness, we are behind the times, especially then in 1985.

The Team examined the field with difficulty as it was still very mushy, uneven and difficult to walk in; they found no depressions or markings. It was not until the summer of 1991 that I was to see the youth. Philip Mantle of BUFORA had interested himself in the case and wrote repeatedly, and eventually the young man agreed to see both him and myself. Accordingly Philip came up to Wales, and drove us to the beautiful Llŷn Peninsular to visit this shy young man, who now was in full employment. I found him difficult to follow, as he was still obviously nervous at

43

recollections of his ordeal, when we tentatively asked if he would be kind enough to take us to the location, he was extremely reluctant, he said he avoided that road at all costs. However, as we had motored a long way to visit him, he did oblige even to the extent of having a few photos taken by me, and then he immediately wanted to leave the spot. We again talked at his place of employment, if he found something too painful to face, his voice would just tail off and he would try to draw the conversation to something else.

Apparently Philip Mantle visited this young man again on his own the following year, I do not know if he was any more lucid then, he later told him he was courting and did not wish to discuss the incident ever again with anyone. In 1994 Philip Mantle and Carl Nagaitis's book was published with quite an accurate account of 'David Thomas', this rather put me off, as I felt an obviously Welsh sounding pseudonym would have been more appropriate, therefore I have given him no name at all! He was totally adamant that his identity never be disclosed.

I was quite surprised that Philip does not mention the youth's descriptions of some of the satellites and planets he saw of our solar system. This is just an ordinary Welsh village boy; he would never have had access to this type of information. When the American Voyager was sending back the fantastic pictures of Ioa, Ganymede and Jupiter's rings, I tried absolutely everywhere to get a book or magazine on the subject, and was looked at with amusement that I should even want such way out matter! I had no success in getting it. The other point I should like to make, is that I doubt if the Policeman, would have quizzed the youth about drugs or drinking, ten years ago in this area of North Wales this point would have been irrelevant. In any case this policeman would have either known or knew of this youth, his family and everyone else on his beat. We are talking about rural Wales - everybody knows everybody and the police and everybody else did give lifts as matter of course to people. I regret to say this open trust is gradually changing only in the last couple of years, and such seaside towns as Rhyl, Colwyn Bay and others do now have minor drugs problem. Minor in comparison with major English cities, and such places as Cardiff.

NOTE: *Investigators - Contact International UK Headquarters team, Philip Mantle, Margaret Fry*

Surrey, England

The first report I ever received of Humanoids was from Roy Fisher of Purley the Contact International investigator mentioned in my book Link to the Stars. I had with difficulty crossed London by train and bus to visit him, expecting to be told of such unusual things as strange lights or objects in the sky, what I got just about blew my

44

mind! Nowadays most people know through reading about CE3 and CE4 cases, but not so in 1977 in Britain, more especially animal mutilations had never been thought of in the area I lived then, of North Kent.

Roy told me that he was doing an Investigation of two boys in Kenley, Surrey and I could go with him if I wished. Unfortunately I was unable to undertake such a complicated long journey cross country, but this is what I recall being told. Robert or Keith, or both lived at the edge of a disused wartime American airport; the tarmac and runways were overgrown and corroded by couch grass, though still visible. On more than one occasion the boys had seen bright lights come down on to these runways, and standing by the patio doors or going down to the bottom of the garden, they had flashed signals to the lights. When the lights responded, they got quite a fright, so that their parents warned them not to do this again. This occurred about September 1977.

Months later at Christmas the boys who were about 15 years of age and friends, were being left on their own in the house, when their parents went out. These lights, silvery orange-yellow and saucer-shaped, again came down and landed on the disused runway. At this the boys reminded each other that they had promised not to flash their torches and stay indoors. But eventually curiosity got the better of Keith and he went from the kitchen door at the side of the house to the back garden, he came face to face with a man standing near his guinea-pig cage. He described him as being at least 6 to 7 ft. tall, wearing a suit like astronauts wear, he could see no zips or fastenings, and his shoes were part of the suit, his hair was shoulder length and sandy, he had a very long forehead, he was not wearing a helmet or anything on his head. His eyes were blue around the pupil, but the actual pupil was red. His eyes were very penetrating and he stared at the boy. He wore a wide belt which was white. This was 6.30p.m. on Christmas Day. At this Keith turned and fled indoors, bolting the door, and he and Robert hid under the bed upstairs until the parents came home.

On Boxing Day at the same time 6.30pm the 26th December, the boys saw two small people looking through the kitchen window, they were exactly the same in appearance and clothing as the tall Being the previous day, again the boys ran away and hid, all the doors were already bolted. When the parents came home, this time they went to the police who told them several people, mostly children had given reports of these UFOs coming down on the Kenley runways seen from different angles from all the houses backing on to this disused airport.

The police examined Keith's guinea-pig which had been neatly slit open from under the mouth to its genitals, there was no blood, but claw marks as though it had gone mad to get out. I do not recall how Roy heard of this, he was able to interview the boys shortly after, and got their parents' permission for them to take him to the runways to show where the lights came down. There were burn marks of 40ft on the disused runway, and at the side the carcass of a fox, which had been neatly slit open also, with parts of it missing. I was shown photos of all this. There were so many questions begging to be asked and bits of vital investigation left out. I say all this with hindsight, I am sure Roy Fisher did his best and none of us had any experience in those days with these humanoid cases.

Plumstead Common, London SE18 - 17th July 1978

Plumstead Common, London SE18 Monday the 17th July 1978 7.45p.m. A fine sunny evening, no winds, no clouds, the sunset at 9.10p.m. So that it was as clear as daylight. Mrs Mary .... an Irish lady with 5 children, lived with her husband in a large Victorian house leading down from the Common, one of hundreds of similar ones, all terraced and forming a large part of the area, which in a crowded city, the only green being the Common.

That warm July evening she was walking her dog accompanied by two daughters; they were crossing the Common by an artificial small pond, as the children and dog ran ahead. Mary decided to sit down for a while on the grass near to a small copse of trees. Two main roads leading to Woolwich are on either side of this, and although the roads are bordered by trees on the park side, the clump of trees screening the pond are plainly visible from these busy roads.

Suddenly Mary saw a large orange ball of light hurtle from the sky, and land in front of this copse. Being no more than yards from it Mary was shocked and still more so when two small men emerged from this walking towards her. Then glancing to a side, she perceived her father sitting on the ground beside her. Her Father had been dead six years! As the men approached she saw that they were quite small about 3ft to 4ft dressed like chauffeurs in peaked caps and fawn coloured uniforms, which had raised gadgets down the front of the chest in pairs. They attempted to talk to her, but this is where she passed clean out.

The next thing she recalled seeing was her husband anxiously bending over her; he and the children had been searching for her, when she did not return for a considerable time. He lifted her, put her in their car, and drove her to the hospital nearby down the hill. There, Mary remained for several weeks, being treated firstly for severe shock, later being seen by a psychiatrist. At first she was unable to see at all for three months, she had a rash on her face and arms and all the exposed parts of her body. She lost an entire week after coming around to consciousness and was in terrible pain, as the Beings had approached her, she had felt all the energy drain from her body and her blood surge down to her feet. Almost word for word what Jean Hingley was to tell me six months later.

Thereafter they had all sorts of paranormal experiences in their house, heard and felt by both her and the children; they would hear their Mother's name being called loudly. Although she was treated for psychiatric disorder, no regard was paid at all to the physical symptoms Mary suffered, at the end the psychiatrist admitted there was nothing wrong with Mary, she had had an experience that he did not understand, but which he felt could be real, so they left her to it. Because their children attended the name nursery school, Mary, Dave and Rose Chatterton met. They had heard of her experience, and wanting to help invited her to their home to look at their books, their UFO reports to see that she was one of thousands of people worldwide who had lived through this type of experience. For a while this helped, but the doctors at the hospital did not take kindly to the UFO explanation, as the cause of her ills, she was still wearing dark glasses when they knew her. Unfortunately shortly after they moved down to the coast, so did not know what became of Mary. She was invited to continue with seeing me, but the Doctors had succeeded in making her lose the little faith she had in UFO investigators.

Report—Extra!

Presented by Norman Oliver

Margaret Fry, an investigator of long standing for Contact UK and also a Bufora member, has kindly given me permission to publish details of this intriguing CBIII case which bears some similarities to a report I referred to in a Kensington talk last year; it is also of interest to me personally since I know the area concerned extremely well.—Ed.

On the Common . . . . .

Location: Plumstead Common,
           London, SE18

Date: Monday 17 July 1978

Time: 7.45pm. Conditions: A fine
           sunny evening (sunset: 9.10
           pm); no wind: no clouds.

In March this year, Margaret Fry gave me the following account of the experience of the witness—who I shall refer to as Mrs M. . . .

The witness is still in such a nervous state over the occurrence that she refuses to allow her full name to be used: several visits took place with her. Mrs M is 36 years old, has five children and lives with her husband on one of the roads leading down from Plumstead Common. The houses on these roads are continuous, terraced, large and roomy Victorian houses.

That July evening, she was taking her two daughters and the family dog for a walk on the Common, and as they were returning home, Mrs M decided to sit down for a while on the grass in a spot a few yards from a small copse of trees. A narrow road cuts across the Common just past this clump and a major thoroughfare passes right over the main plateau of the Common to Woolwich: the clump of trees is clearly visible from both. The witness, how-

ever, did not recall whether much—or indeed any, traffic was around.

Suddenly, the witness related, a large orange ball of light hurtled out of the sky towards the clump of trees. This ball settled on the grass on the Common side, beside the trees and Mrs M, by now in a shocked state, watched two small men walking towards her. Then, glancing to her side, she saw her father—who had been dead six years—sitting beside her on the grass wearing a suit. She looked again towards the approaching men, who now appeared to her to be near 5 feet in height, though her first impression had been nearer 3 feet. They were dressed like chauffeurs in peaked caps and fawn uniforms, with raised gadgets or buttons down the front of the chests. They stood in front of her and talked, but she could not understand them. She must then have passed out in fright.

The next thing she was aware of was her husband getting her into their car and of being driven to hospital. Mrs M remained there for several weeks and, indeed, continued to receive treatment for about ten months afterwards. At first, she could not set at all—her sight was lost for about three months. At the beginning she had a rash on her face and arms, all the exposed areas of her body. In her own words, she 'lost an entire week *after* the incident', and was in terrible pain. When she saw the beings come towards her she says she felt all the energy drain out of her body and the blood go down to her feet, leaving her very cold.

Since this occurrence, her daughter J—and she have felt a 'presence' in the house on occasion. The two

daughters (14 years old), one other daughter and the two sons have on occasion heard their mother's name being called, and other odd occurrences have taken place which the witness feels too nervous to talk about.

Though at first treated in hospital for 'nerves,' later, the psychiatrist who treated her decided that she had not had a nervous breakdown, but had had some sort of experience which he did not understand, but which he thought to be quite real. Neither those at the hospital nor the witness herself had previously given any attention to the subject of UFOs and little attention was given to the physical symptoms that accompanied her distressed mental state, which was made worse by neither she nor the doctors being able to relate her experience to a physical one within the framework of their own knowledge.

Coincidentally, on coming out of hospital, she met two people interested

in UFOs—both she and they had a child attending the same nursery school—who tried to reassure her by telling her of similar experiences claimed by others worldwide. Though at first retired, she found that doctors at the hospital did not take kindly to UFOs as a possible cause of her condition and again became unhappy and nervous. Her eyesight has never fully recovered and she still wears dark glasses.

     *   *   *   *

The case of the expanding UFO: Or . . . . ?

Our next report was received from author and former Bufora RIC Randall Jones Pugh, who considers it indicates there is a psychic, unstable and invisible, body of 'captured', capable of capturing the intellect and body of an individual, suggesting that 'malevolent traits' may be manifested. At the family's request, their names and location details have been omitted

continued overleaf

11

Extract from BUFORA Journal 1978 describing Mrs. M's experiences

10

Ernie and Gwylim - Mynydd Hiraethog Moors,Clwyd, North Wales 1966

The road from Cerrigydrudion to Ruthin is the B 5l05. At Cerrigydrudion a lonely small village at the tail end of the Denbigh Moor, the road forks to the right you wind up to a lonely pub called The Crops Keys, this forks off again to narrow country roads which eventually lead to y Cyffylliog a small hamlet in the centre of the Hiraethog Moors where Ernie spent his childhood. The hamlet and the area are not so far as the crow flies to Worlds End, where there is a vast underground military base in a very isolated area.

From Ruthin where Ernie worked at R. Ellis & Sons, Ernie then a young lad of 16/17 years used to walk the 5 miles home. It was his habit to call in the off-licence of The Bridge Hotel in Bontuchel to collect a packet of five Woodbine cigarettes every evening before continuing on his homeward walk. He noted the time, it was 7.05 pm by the clock there. There was a small Saw Mill at Bontuchel which he passed to get on to a beautiful secluded road, a five mile stretch with forests on one side, sometimes both sides of the road, at the bottom of which a river runs on one side, this is all on very high grounds of the Moors, and eventually goes to the hamlet of Cyssylliog. The chance that you will pass another car or vehicle at any time of the year is pretty unlikely. If you do, it is an event and generally one of your fellow villagers or some farmer you know.

It took Ernie a bit over 10 minutes to reach this lonely stretch of road from The Bridge Hotel, Bontuchel. On this narrow but good surface road through a forest in a narrow valley, then you came to a small bridge, beyond this a further straight mile through this valley, and as far back in time every Villager can remember on which strange paranormal things have happened. The whole District knows about this and it is important to note, that because of this, what happened to Ernie and Gwylim was accepted by people. Nobody disbelieved them or made fun. At the time Ernie was sixteen years of age Gwylim whom he knew of because he used to see him in his truck, was barely an acquaintance and much older 30 something years of age, he thought.

To mention some of the strange happenings, in 1965 a driver shot off the road into a tree, as this mile stretch of road is fairly wide for North Wales rural areas, flat, straight and well maintained, there was no other traffic coming, or on the road. A lorry landed in a hedge at the same spot, vehicles have frequently gone off the road at this spot for no apparent reason. Ernie's own sister-in-law saw a figure crossing the road at it. Engines cut out for no apparent reason. A brother-in-law's son Ron was in his small Mini on the same stretch of road one evening, when his lights cut out as a big figure on a horse passed him by. He was so afraid, he abandoned the car and raced all the way home to the village, as these incidents went on into the 1970s and later, it was after

Ernie's and Gwylim's event which he thinks took place in 1967. He cannot now remember the year exactly, for he has since survived a serious car crash and other illnesses.

In late 1989 or 1990 we went with Ernie to this locality and my local researcher and friend Margaret Hainge-Lloyd, audio taped him on the spot. At that time he had a better recollection of dates and times and he felt the event took place in 1963. This is only relevant to our UFO research and records, but Ernie does recall exactly what happened very vividly. When he got to the spot where there is a small tree the other side of the low hawthorn hedge before the bridge - he was startled to see a small George Adamski type craft come over the forested area into the valley. As it approached it was swaying gently from side to side, like a falling leaf. This thoroughly alarmed him and he ran into the centre of the road looking wildly about for some means of escape. To his immense relief he saw and heard a wagon approaching down the road, he flagged it down and jumped in without looking to see who was driving. When he did look, he realised it was an acquaintance Gwylim, whom he knew had a wife working in Denbigh Hospital as a nurse. This man possibly also lived in the town of Denbigh but he did not know his surname. That was all he knew by hearsay about him. With his finger shaking he pointed out the craft that was approaching, and now positioned itself right over the bonnet of the vehicle. They both yelled in terror.

The next thing that either were aware of, was that they were miles past Cyssylliog towards the crossroads of the A 525/A5104 where Stephen was later abducted off his motorcycle in 1979. It was pitch dark there being no road lights in that remote area. Gwylim turned around and they went back to Ernie's hamlet y Gyffylliog where his Mother was anxiously waiting, he being home so late back from work. When I met Ernie in 1988 and he described all this I took a lot of notes, he told me he though he had arrived home about 1 am or so. When we later audio taped him in 1990 he though it may have been 9 pm. They probably did not look at the time; they had been through a traumatising experience and were tired and afraid. With the passage of years such exact details have been forgotten. The point is they had lost several hours they were not aware of at the time. In addition a month later Ernie had a red rash from head to toe which blistered, itched and was painful. He went to his Doctor, this rash then came and went appearing in spring, disappeared in summer and maybe reappeared in autumn /winter. He was given a smoothing ointment and it went after a year He was left with a brown mark on his side towards the back, which he did not have before, and for awhile after he felt he had a stone just under the skin of his lip. This eventually went. He did not know what happened to Gwylim, as he did not keep in touch with him. Was this man abducted with Ernie? Unless we find him again we will not know.

From a psychologist's point of view I would say Ernie's case is extremely interesting. I have known him from the 1980's; various Welsh friends from the same area have known Ernie since school days. So for the first few years after the experience Ernie did not follow the pattern of most people who feel they are abductees, he was still living in the area amongst friends and acquaintances, he was accepted, particularly in view of the fact that others had paranormal experiences in the same spot. Although he knew he had lost some hours of times, this aspect of it hardly was considered.

By the time I met Ernie in about 1987/88, he had reached the stage of feeling he wanted hypnotic regressions, because he had again had a close sighting of a UFO, which renewed his desire to know exactly what happened the first time. Unlike most people it was just a burning curiosity, not fear, he had never had nightmares, this I felt was because in his community he and his experience were accepted. In later years he got a job in a Hospital as an ambulance man, and here for the first time his attitude changed. He lived in fear of his bosses finding out and did not want to discuss the incident at all, at the time unemployment in Wales was particularly high under the Conservative Government, so his fears were justified.

As my friend and long time partner in Ufology Alan Hilton professional hypnotist says most people who seriously investigate the abduction mystery desperately try to find alternative, natural explanations, finding solace in Known sciences and psychology. Abductees are instinctively aware of the reality of their experiences, so they find these answers destructive and unacceptable to them, so they turn to occult, channelling, spiritualists, and believe me these groups of people get far more abductees turning to them, than we down-to-earth so called scientifically orientated UFO investigators. If we want to really understand this phenomenon we should be aware of this trend and realise we have to listen more, cooperate and combine to meet the needs of abductees far more. There are people who are advancing hallucinatory abduction experiences activated in the percipient's brain by electrical impulses. Firstly, earth bound geological processes that create a luminous phenomenon which in turn releases an electromagnetic effect to the temporal lobe structure to the witnesses brain, which in turn causes them to "believe they see extraterrestrial craft," (apart from abductions). In the first instance a great number of people all over the world have seen actual nuts and bolts crafts, I have, not lights in the night sky, this includes air pilots. To suggest that these responsible people, who carry the lives of hundreds in their capable hands and brains, are being temporally affected and collectively, for whole crews report these sightings, is truly arrogant. A whole crew of highly responsible trained people are temporally affected by electromagnetic fields, high up above the earth's atmosphere, and are then according to these sceptics, in a hallucinatory condition, in which there is no objective reality, and no control of themselves, let alone their trusting passengers! How can thinking people credit these crackpot ideas? Why not just accept that this is a technology way in advance, hundreds of years ahead of us, that we can at present have no explanation for in our present scientific knowledge.

Why too are these triggered hallucinations all following the same pattern, be they in Bhutan, Madagascar, the U.S.A Europe and Greenhithe, Kent, England where Marie Ward who believed she was an abductee, a highly intelligent totally sincere young woman, who believed fervently she should let people know. For her pains she agreed to go on a television programme. She was then humiliated by television personalities who have never troubled to learn anything about the UFO phenomenon and subjected by proponents of fanciful theories with more holes than a sieve, as being a charlatan? Small wonder few abductees ever want publicity or have the urge to tell people, and we in the Ufology world are the losers. People from all over the world with totally different cultures and backgrounds cannot relate the same abduction scenario, without there being some reality to a frightening shared experience, for if we listen carefully the same threads run through all these cases. We should, if we had the guts, bring this to the attention and study of the medical profession at large, if and where possible.

A couple of years ago Ernie was driving an ambulance when a portocabin came loose from its moorings on a vehicle in front of them and crashed down to the side of the ambulance. Ernie was very badly injured and had to get early retirement from work. Since being in retirement he has had time to reflect on what happened that night so many years ago, he has by conscious regression felt he was in fact taken into this small Adamski like craft. He vaguely recalls the smell of burning rubber, seeing Beings similar to humans, of his height 5ft 11 inches, or a bit taller, and they had grey skins. He thinks they gave him the usual medical type of examination, and conversed with him telepathically. Whether this is a jumble of what he may have read since or seen on television, and a mixture of what may have really happened to him, who is to say. All I know is we have known him for years and he is a perfectly sincere person, like the dozens and dozens of others I have met and tried to help over the years, who are trying to find some answers to their own frightening experience with only support from a very few UFO researchers and none at all from the professions in authority or armchair researchers.

Investigators - Margaret Fry, Margaret Hainge-Lloyd, John Roberts

Stephen - World's End, Denbigh Moors, North Wales

Then aged about 19 years Stephen was on his motor-bike on the A5104 just past the Horseshoe Pass and Bryneglwys to the cross roads of A5251/A5104.

It was about mid-night and he had just dropped his then girlfriend home, and was returning to his own house, when he saw a bright white light in the sky, it was gradually and slowly coming down. He then saw it slowly receding, and looking around was puzzled. The area is a very lonely mysterious looking place even in daylight with absolutely no houses, not even scattered farms, for miles. It is near an area called World's End and for good reason, it seems like it, it is so isolated. However there is a very secret Military base set several miles into wooded area further up this local road. Now Stephen looked around and found he was no longer coming to the cross-roads, but a couple of miles past them, it was no longer pitch dark, dawn was breaking, and his motor-bike lay on its side by the roadside, this road is very narrow anyway.

This occurred whilst Stephen was still 18 in 1979, but he does not recall the month, he was now standing puzzled in the road past a hamlet called Pen-y-stryl, when he got home he noted it was 5.00a.m. His Mother was quite upset, saying she had waited up thinking he had had an accident, he then went off to bed. At the time Stephen worked for the Water Board laying pipes, this was the reason why he was on that lonely road, not many people, even local people take it at night, there are other longer but less lonely roads. Stephen had been working in the Military campus, and therefore used this road frequently and thought nothing about using it at night. He told me that the Military base was so secret, that Military guards ensured that all the Water Board men did not stray into areas where they were prohibited.

After this puzzling incident of time loss, Stephen started having nightmares, which he tried to shove to the recesses of his mind. At times he had tried to tell his family or friends of these missing hours, but they all derided him. He later met another girl, they got married, mortgaged a house, had two children, and in the stage his life is at when I met him, he has a wife, two small children and had just been made redundant, the usual story today.

A few years after this incident Stephen, who had tried in vain to shove vague memories into the background, decided his Life was not going in the right direction, so he decided to do something about it. He knew these memories connected to a UFO, a light that came down to him, so he decided to try and find some UFO books to read. but this proved difficult. Then in 1993 quite by chance he heard a Radio talk, during which listeners were told that victims of UFO abductions could call BUFORA's phone number, and contact the Victim Support Group. He did phone this number, and got Mrs. Phillips, Ken's wife who told him he was out and to ring again in the evening, but this slight set back put him off, he was feeling very nervous about approaching anyone. So virtually a year went by before he plucked up the courage to ring Ken Phillips' number again. This time he got Ken, who kindly explained he was too far to help him, but to contact Margaret Fry in his area, giving him my telephone number. This time he decided it was now or never so rang me immediately.

Even so it took many sympathetic phone calls before Stephen could bring himself to come to my house, he could drive and had a car, I can't, he was then living in Holywell, so I had to encourage him to come over and I wouldn't eat him, I was just an ordinary elderly lady with grandchildren etc! We talked of his children. Eventually he came on the 2nd November 1994. Stephen had reached a stage where he felt he had to have hypnotic regression to lay his fears; he was still having periodic nightmares. I rang and asked Mary Nightingale a professional hypnotist I know, but she was too expensive, Stephen was now out of a job. At this I contacted my good friend Alan Hilton, he was due to visit me on the 6th November so we agreed for Stephen to come to my house on Wednesday the 7th November at 11.30a.m. Stephen arrived promptly and after tea and a relaxing conversation agreed to a gentle hypnotic session. He was very apprehensive and Alan had to give him relaxation and reassurances, eventually the sessions ended past 1.00pm when I suggested lunch, and change, but by now Stephen only wanted to talk about a release of memories, he wanted to do drawings. Stephen is perfectly normal but a somewhat shy person.

This is what transpired that night in 1979. He remembered dropping his motor-cycle on the side of the road, he then encountered a thick black wall, but the next recollection is of lying on a table absolutely terrified, a tall very thin man with a long face, pointed eyes, no hair and a very long bluish/yellow body was looking down at him. This creature appeared to have no clothes on; his body was more like a transparent fish. Not a ghost Stephen emphasised, for the body had substance, it was matter but the sort you can see through, like clear Perspex or whatever. This Being had long arms, which were very thin, and at the end of these were long thin fingers, three fingers to each hand, the knuckles were very prominent. He noted all these tiny details, as he was too afraid to take in the whole. He realised he had floated into this room; now he noted there were three small Beings standing alongside by the table he was on. They too had similar faces and very thin bodies. One of these little Beings held what appeared to be a gun ray, with lights coming from it shining into his eyes. He felt this was to examine the inside of his head, rather than his eyes. Further into the room he now noted was a

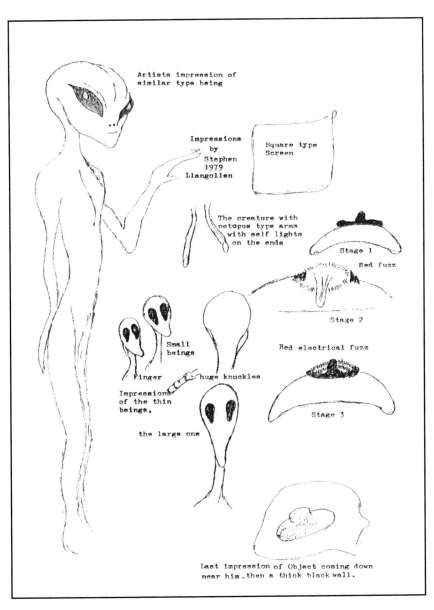

Artists impression of
similar type being

Impressions
by
Stephen
1979
Llangollen

Square type
Screen

The creature with
octopus type arms
with self lights
on the ends

Stage 1

Red fuzz

Stage 2

Small
beings

Red electrical fuzz

Finger   huge knuckles

Impressions
of the thin
beings,

Stage 3

the large one

Last impression of Object coming down
near him_then a thick black wall.

Stephen's impressions of the Beings he saw in 1979

Creature which had two long arms like an octopus. At the end of each of these were lights. Artificial light I queried?

No, said Stephen more like our glow-worms, the light was part of its body. These arms kept reaching out to near his body, and it then came into his head, he was there for genetic purposes. He felt still more terrified wondering what they would do next. He became aware of a long central column up the centre of the room he was in, which had some sort of electrical activity at the top which was rotating, there also appeared to be compartments leading off from this room, which had doors that moved up and down to open, there appeared to be no motivating controls or engines etc. in this room he was in, he tried to concentrate on these details to calm himself, he could not move. He then noted another Being standing behind a screen, he could only see him from the shoulders up, and he appeared to be controlling things. This line of thought was not pursued by the hypnotist, as Stephen was now very agitated about a tunnel of honeycomb he could see, there were various things in it, but he became vague and tailed off, at this point Alan felt the session should come to an end, as his patient was obviously distressed. He asked if he could see his motor-bike and Stephen said vaguely 'its at the side of the road, there is a black wall.' At this he brought him out of the trance.

I have had a number of conversations with Stephen since, sometimes he remembers some small detail further, he also wants further sessions, as he goes through patches when he still has nightmares, then for a while he forgets and his life goes on in an even keel. He now has a job, his house was repossessed, and he is living in rented accommodation. In other words life goes on, but Stephen still has ghosts to lay, he knows this, so the sessions are not over.

I think this new network of National Victim Support will eventually be of great support to people like Stephen, as professional psychologists and hypnotists are gradually in small numbers joining it, but I was encouraged by what Professor John Mack said to me, 'don't underestimate yourself, life and your experiences with this work have made you a professional, you help these people, lend a sympathetic ear, so a Counsellor is every bit as important as the professional'.

Regretfully I have to say it is now 2004 and Professor John Mack's National Victim Support has not progressed at all in the UK.

The Beach, Pensarn , Abergele, North Wales late September from about 2.10 am 1973.

There were four UFOS involved in this very strange experience. Tim (pseudonym) was a young man at the time and his friends from school days, John and Alun (pseudonyms) whom he met from time to time but was not intimately friendly with. They were gathered together and discussed such things as ghost and oujii boards on this occasion, after which they decided it might be fun to spend that summer's night on the beach.   They settled themselves down on a bench on Pensarn Beach, which was surrounded by a plastic and wood shelter. They had had not seen Alun for awhile, so they sat chatting to about 12 midnight when John and Alun fell asleep, Tim continued to take an interest in everything around him, the sea, beach area, there was a full moon and some stars visible, the night was very calm with the sky a dull light navy blue, no clouds anywhere. Round about 2 am Tim noticed a single white/yellow cloud like oval in the distance over the Irish Sea. This then floated slowly towards the beach, it was not very high in the sky and seemed to him to be about 200 ft by 100 ft in size and as it came nearer it was bright white/yellow. It gradually passed right over them, and quite low over the beach, floating on towards the residential part of the town behind them and he wondered what it could be. There is a large park and fields towards the beach, unlike most seaside places the houses are at least a 1/2 mile from the sea. This unusual lit- up cloud then just stopped over Abergele Police Station, which Tim who had got up to follow it, thought quite strange. How could a cloud just stop floating and hover?

It then started coming back to the beach area which rather alarmed Tim, for it was now almost directly over and he tried to awaken his friend John, but he began to feel annoyed because there seemed to be two invisible pillars of some power that prevented him from doing this. Then he tried to awake Alun and the same force stopped him. So he started yelling, the cloud like thing then carried on out to sea, once it receded he was able to shake his friends awake. He told his friends, but they disbelieved him and said they wanted to sleep. He asked them to stay awake at least the next 10 minutes to see what would happen next. The whole sighting had lasted about half an hour. In fact it was about 10 minutes later that John noticed three gigantic grey/black ovals coming from the direction of Rhyl down the coast line, they were drifting no more than 500ft up, judging by the width that spread over to the large Victorian buildings on the other side of the main road, they thought them several hundred feet across. Alun who was sitting on the bench did not appear to notice, but these two watched these three Objects come steadily on until they passed them on the beach at an angle of 50 degrees. When they reached Pensarn railway station the leading Object stopped, and the one behind went right into it and merged, ditto the third one. Once they all merged they twisted and turned and seemed to churn up dull colours of green, blue, yellow and red. That went on for about 15 minutes, after which it stopped and went back to a very black

57

cloud like Object. The rest of the sky was by now fairly light with no clouds, as this thing started to drift again towards them on the beach

As this Object came towards them Tim and John got behind between the half shelter and the bench, whilst Alun sat on, he could not see anything and thought they were behaving stupidly. Then this Object came down very low over the shelter, so that it blacked out the sky and light, they were so afraid they prayed aloud. After a few minutes the Object receded and went up at an angle on the Pensarn/Kinmel bay side. Alun had got up and was staring in the direction the craft was going, yet once it had gone he turned to the other two and said "Whatever is the matter with you two, I can't see anything".

Tim made the comment to me, that this friend of theirs had always been very matter-of-fact and totally insensitive to paranormal feelings since they had been children, he just could not envisage such phenomena as ghosts or anything out of the ordinary. They had never been particularly close friends he said. Yet it is interesting that they shared the effects of this experience. For about 10 minutes after the Object left all three felt a burning of the skin on their faces and the tops of their hands. They were in such pain they at first thought of rushing into the sea, but then reasoned the salt water would aggravate the burning, so decided to use tap water to wash themselves. According to Tim they did not go immediately but talked and debated on the beach for another hour before walking to the Railway station. As the whole incident had taken an hour, this brought the time to about 4.10 am, naturally the Station was closed. They then walked back to the beach and fell asleep on the bench. About 6 am they were woken by the Police. They explained that they had just wanted the adventure of spending the night out and this was accepted in those happy drug free days in North Wales. Now regrettably this lovely, mostly rural mountainous area has caught up with the rest of the British Isles, and no respectable person ventures on to Pensarn beach after dark, all sorts of unsavoury dealers meet there, there was even a murder reported in all the national newspapers a few years ago. Shortly after the Police left the three men walked to Bunties Cafe near the Beach, it was closed, they knew they would have to wait till about 7 am/8 am for the Cafe people to arrive. Then they decided to go back to the beach.

This is Tim's story, given to me with the uttermost care and detail for he says it has been in his memory ever since, it will never go away. It is as clear today as it was at the time. He has carefully worked out the times of each section of the incident, which I would query although I am sure this happened as he relates. He worked out that the first UFO incident lasted 29 minutes, and so on, he felt he could account for all the time, but he says he did not know if he had a watch on! I have considered these points -

58

- Abergele, Kinmel Bay, Rhyl etc, are all seaside resorts to the Irish Sea of course.

- John did not see the first cloud-like object, it seems though he was looking out to the sea when it was receding in the distance.

- The pillars of power - Tim said he sensed an intelligence coming from them, it was a power that seemed to him to be forceful and overpowering, but not frightening. When it receded and he was allowed to awake his companions, they naturally told him he must have been dreaming, but he is quite adamant he never went to sleep, except after they had been to the railway station and everything was locked up

- When the three UFOS merged, the first one remained the same size.

- The burning effects lasted two to three days for all three young men.

Why would they, when they were feeling burnt, debate for an hour before going to see if any place was open so that they could wash with tap water? The first time Tim told me about this, he thought they went to the Railway Station at about 5.30 am and then straight on to Bunties Cafe, this seemed to me a more logical course of the events after the departure of the UFO. This would have seemed to imply that he could not really account for about two hours after the Object left. A couple of weeks later after giving it much thought, he came back and said no, this was not correct. They had debated for an hour and then went to the Station at 4.10 am. This again seemed illogical to me, for if your face and hands are burning, the first thing you would want to instinctively do, would be to wash the burning sensation away as soon as possible. Having read that other abductees have felt controlled by Alien intelligences, I wondered if the same thing happened to them, and he is not now really aware of the sequence of events after the UFO left. Maybe they were induced to fall asleep without realising how long this lasted.

I did of course ask why they had not simply gone home to wash. He said all their parents shut the doors at about midnight and after that would not let them in. Tim himself had very conventional strict parents and he would not have dared to go home at that hour of the morning, still less tell his parents about his strange experience. They did talk of this and the primary consideration was that they were afraid to walk along the unlit very long coastal road, which was quite a distance from their homes and the direction in which the last huge grey/black UFO had gone.

I also asked what Alun's reaction was to them all being burnt simultaneously, when he appeared to have seen nothing. He said they were so thunderstruck themselves they did not notice, but they did meet from time to time at other teenager's houses, his own parents would not have his friends over. When they did meet, they did tell their friends about this experience. They did debate too as to whether they should inform R.A.F Valley at Anglesey, but felt too afraid that they would not be believed and it would cause them trouble. They were round about 17/18 years of age when this happened and gradually over the years as they courted, then married they had lost touch. Since discussing all this with me, he felt he should try to trace John and would endeavour to do so.

Until he came to me Tim had read no UFO books, he had seen a TV UFO programme. I asked him if it would help him to better understand what had happened to them if I lent him some carefully selected books. He said that would be very much appreciated, as he wanted to understand what it was all about. In my view helping these victims who come to us for comfort and advice is far more important than any research. Our first concern should be the witnesses, for without these people there would be no Ufology research. So did they have some missing time, it is very difficult to judge this after such a length of time, especially as it would not have occurred to the witnesses to make notes in 1973 when this happened. I think it sufficiently strange to include in this Chapter.

Further Tim did mention that he saw something very strange and unaccountable as a 12 year old boy on the marshes between Kinmel Bay/Rhuddlan, which is very flat land going towards the estuary that outlets at Rhyl harbour. It is rather dull scenery of flat fields surrounded by hedges, and he was looking for bird's nests in the hedgerows that surrounded the fields, taking a very narrow track farmers use. He saw a very small strange looking Object in the centre of an enclosed field, which took up into the sky, it left a trail of fire similar to a fire rocket, with the same sound, as a child he thought this really weird and unaccountable! He does not now remember exactly what it looked like, it was less than a foot in size, but that was all he has ever seen prior to the beach incident.

A further interview Tim told me he had seen a number of ghosts of dead relatives in his childhood, and experienced paranormal events some with his younger brother. On one occasion he and his brother had been put to bed when they saw their grandmother come into the room holding the hand of a man they did not know, they could see through them. They ran down the stairs to their parents, but he said his father had always been very harsh, and he yelled at them to go back to bed immediately. Yet his grandmother was very much alive at the time and visiting them regularly and normally.

I asked if he associated these events with what happened to him and his friends on the beach. He said he felt that UFOS and what we consider paranormal exist in the same dimension. I have expressed my feelings on this elsewhere in the book.

Of course over the years I have read in Flying Saucer Review and other magazines from Australia, the USA and Britain, and had some personal reports previously of one person seeing something or having an experience, that someone close by has no idea of, it is most unusual though for the unaware person to have the same effects as the person undergoing the experience. Tim who did not want his name known would like to hear from other people or researchers who know of something similar.

The Pentre Halkyn Contactee Mrs Irene Williams 1982

I got to know of Mrs Irene Williams through a mutual acquaintance who had lived in Crowborough, Sussex and retired to Pentre Halkyn. We spoke for quite some time on the phone before meeting. When we did meet in 1986 I found Irene was one of the most sensible, happy, outgoing, well-balanced middle-aged ladies one could ever hope to meet. Her husband was retired and they were a compatible couple, they had a large family of sons, daughters-in-law and grandchildren living around their area who frequently visited, plus a teenage son, for whose friends they kept open house. Irene was well known in Pentre Halkyn and lived in a large old farm house dating from the 16th/17th century called The White House, Irene took part in village life and her Church activities

It is a fallacy to imagine contactees are maladjusted people, most are very ordinary human beings. Here I should say that because so many people in Pentre Halkyn had seen UFOS, to mention a Council worker who one morning saw a green coloured craft sitting on the Church roof in November 1982; so the villagers certainly did not disbelieve what happened to Irene, extraordinary as it was.

So to say Irene wanted anonymity is quite incorrect, she wanted people to know, as she felt everyone should realise Aliens were coming to our planet Earth. Some years before her husband who had worked in a factory on the Coast had gone outside during a tea break. A large bright green cigar shaped craft passed very low and slowly over the building, he called out to his work mates, but all they did was deride him. I don't suppose it even occurred to Irene to contact a newspaper, and I certainly never suggested it, as I knew the pressure people could be put to with publicity of this sort. Irene certainly wanted all her acquaintances and any people who were interested to know about her experience.

On the 30th January 1986 two taxi drivers were parked in different roads of Connah's Quay, when two small odd shaped craft passed just less than 100 ft over the bonnets of their taxis, this seen by everyone else on the street. They were small, metallic and best described as tall, rounded welsh hats, with long rectangular windows that were softly lit up. The Evening Leader wrote of this event. These two men had heard "through the grape vine" of Mrs Williams and were anxious to meet her after their own experiences. They contacted me (all my details are kept in various Libraries in North Wales) and said they would like to meet her, so I asked them if they would motor me to Pentre Halkyn. We then arranged a visit. With typical Welsh hospitality Irene had prepared an enormous high Tea for us, and two of her acquaintances who had seen UFOS and wanted to meet me joined us, as we sat around and got acquainted.

Irene then told us all that on the 12th July 1982 at 11.25 pm. she had been caring for her son's dog whilst his family went on holiday. The dog was sitting in the front porch room that was like a conservatory. She went to call him in when she was rooted to the spot in terror, for hurtling towards her was what she took to be a meteorite. It abruptly stopped over a tree above the bungalow roof of her neighbour. Her neighbour's bungalow was opposite at the top of the steep incline, at the bottom of which was the Williams house. It was making a deep humming sound, was round and virtually yards from Irene. The Object had two rings. The inner ring was dimmer with self-coloured raised knobs dotted about it. The outer ring was much brighter, although it defused no light. Irene tried but her feet seemed glued to the ground, she was so staggered she could not even call out to her husband. When she found she could move, she raced up stairs and looked out of the window, but the Object had gone.

For weeks after this event her eyes were sore and she could hardly keep awake, it affected the dog in the same way. When she described this in the Village Shop a Mrs. Jones said that she too at the same time saw a very large bright green eight-sided Object with hexagonal myriads of lights on it, hovering over the village. Also a Mrs W... had seen the same object floating over the village in broad day light in May 1982. I met this Lady and she said she had remembered the date as she had gone to get her dog from an animal sanctuary, and had been taking it for a walk.

— Irene then told us of how on the 10th November 1983, a Thursday, she had been working very late on some needlework. So as not to disturb her husband she decided to sleep that night in the spare bedroom. She did not settle down well, so got up and went to look out of the window. The house is large and at the base of a steep incline., as described previously. It having been built centuries ago, all the windows were slightly bowed, leaded and very small. She was startled to see a man looking in at her, she irrelevantly thought he had to be on stilts to be level with the first floor window. She noted he had a roundish face, light olive complexion, curly dark short hair, and clothed in an over-all mid-blue boiler type garment. She said she felt a bit startled but not afraid, and then he immediately transferred, or should one say teleported into the room, she did retreat towards her bed, but she asked him if she could touch him as she had to make sure she was not dreaming. He said "put out the light", then he approached her with two fingers in a V sign which he brought close to her eyes, then he vanished. The room turned dark again and she contemplated that he must have been the reason why everything seemed light when he appeared, and she could see his features so distinctly. Only then did she get into bed and fall asleep. In November at 3 am it is dark, and not only Irene, but other witnesses have related the same effect, including myself.

On the 26th July 1978 in Bexleyheath, Kent when thirteen of my neighbours and I watched three black cigar shaped UFOS create a fantastic display of different shaped lights, solely for our benefit for one hour and 26 minutes, the whole of the sky area around them was as light as day, but when they flew away it as suddenly turned dark again. So I knew this could happen when Irene told us of it. In fact so many extraordinary things happened in North Kent during 1978 in what we Ufologists call a 'flap year' when I interviewed 246 people and my husband and I saw UFOS with some of them seven times, that I now know anything is possible when UFOS appear!

Mrs Irene Williams never saw an Alien again. What she did get was what she believed were telepathic messages from Space people. She said she realised that as she had never left North Wales her perceptions of other places which they told her of, could have been too narrow and she could at times misinterpret some of what she received.

She was told of the severe earthquake that took place on the 5th July 1984, the core being at Porthmadog and felt throughout Clwyd. She told everyone of this in June 1984 well before the event. Incidentally throughout the 38 years I have investigated UFOS, I have noted UFOS intensify in the area of earthquakes, shortly before, during and after.

Irene told us that the Space people had told her if she wanted proof of their landing at Pentre Halkyn mountain, she should go and look for three square prod marks their enormous craft had made on landing. Irene had been going up to the mountain since childhood, but she waited until the Spring, as it is dangerous to venture up there in winter. She searched in vain several times then asked her husband to accompany her. Together they looked but did not find the prod marks till April 1984. I do not recall now exactly when they told her they had landed.

Pentre Halkyn has been tunnelled and open-mined for centuries for salt, sulphur, silver, lead and quartz. Even at the time I went there in 1986 they were mining to the right side of the mountain. On the left side facing the Dee Estuary, the whole of the top of the mountain range is a large plateau of deep crevices; disused old dangerous open mine shafts. There are wells covered by only a couple of feet of peat and moss. There are remnants of mediaeval hamlets and villages, Roman road traces, open very large pits strewn with rock fragments and large boulders everywhere. No vehicle could possibly go there, and it is a danger zone for unwary walkers, although locals and tourists do go there in the summer months. During the winter only Quarry men and sheep, and these sheep avoid certain parts. When the Williams did find the three prod squares of roughly 14 inches, placed in a triangle, their minds boggled at the sheer size the craft must have been, as these squares were many yards apart and all in impossible positions, but very clear cut and undisturbed.

Irene took Mr. Jones and Mr. Parker the taxi drivers and myself up to the area. It was a dry, cold and very windy day, very difficult to walk there at all. One of these squares was on the very brink of an open shaft, yet no earth had crumbled away, and it was very puzzling wondering how such a huge craft, which surely was also heavy could have made these indents, which had not altered in spite of heavy winter., rain and snow., and after two whole years when we saw them! A real mystery? The Williams had simply accepted their proof without any questions, they knew no one could conceive them making them themselves, or anybody else with a mechanical digger, the terrain made this totally impossible, even the sheep avoided these open mine shafts. After seeing that impossible evidence, none of us doubted Irene Williams. I paid for this research with a severe attack of bronchitis the following day!

Over the years Irene and I kept in touch. Every time the 'Space people' contacted her, she immediately phoned me. Time and again what they conveyed to her came to pass. A severe flooding in a certain area of France. Once she was told to motor to Llanrwst to fulfil a task. She would not tell me what this was. When I asked why she complied with these sometimes difficult, almost impossible requests, she said they were 'beautiful people', by that she meant they were for the good of mankind. Most impressive was the vivid pictures she was given in her mind of Llandudno being flooded with 30 ft of water, and all down the coast to Ffynnongroyw she saw waves lapping against bungalows. This was a frightening scenario and Irene and I dismissed this as a misinterpretation on her part, it could not possibly happen to the North Wales coastline. It did in the winter of 1991 and took place exactly as she foresaw.
The last time Irene spoke to me over the phone, she was very excited. She had just returned from America where on an internal flight she had looked down through the plane window and seen a perfect circle in a field below. She said "do come over, I have so much to tell you and what I am getting about these corn circles". Unfortunately, for various reasons I was not able to get to Pentre Halkyn, and I did not then hear from Irene for some months. This wasn't unusual, as these telepathic messages came to her spasmodically, sometimes after quite some time. Then an acquaintance who knew Irene came over to tell me she had developed cancer and died. Cancer claims the lives of every second and third person in North Wales and people here blame the Chernobyl disaster and fall out. But I have also noted that people who

get too close to UFOS or encounter humanoids invariably ultimately, if not sooner develop cancer, as I have myself.

On my train journey home that first time I met Irene Williams I examined in my mind the tiny details never written about that people have told me, they all have these common denominators. Alan Hilton of Tunbridge Wells, Kent and I founded the first Victim Support Team in Britain in the early 1970s. He is a physiotherapist, professional hypnotist and an air pilot. This was for people who had either seen humanoids or felt they had been abducted by them. It can be a frightening, mentally scarring experience, and who is there to help them? Doctors? Trained psychiatrists? These professions do not even countenance UFOS exist, let alone people being contacted by aliens. There are still only a handful of Ufologist researchers who specialise in this type of research and help these Victims. For Victims they are of a largely ignorant society about the UFO phenomenon. Alan gave them hypnotherapy if they themselves wanted and asked for it. The majority don't, they just need someone to confide in who will listen with an open mind and heart, as very often their own families reject their experiences as fantasy. Irene Williams was lucky, as her husband had seen a large cigar-shaped fluorescent bright green craft pass low over his head, and when he tried to call out to his work mates he was derided, so as he told me he wasn't about to deride his wife's experiences, so not only he but her whole family believed her.

That January 1986 as I sat in the train returning home I thought of –

Mrs Ellen Howson 1967. During a violent storm a UFO passed over their house roof and landed on the back lawn. Next morning there was a deep circular indent there full of fluorescent blue rainwater. The children put on wellington boots and happily splashed in. We both worked for the London Borough of Greenwich local government then, and when she told me of this, I felt horrified and told her to bathe them carefully and not go in the back garden at all for a while.
Colin Crowhurst 1971. A well qualified pilot had a Being enter his bed room and look at him then vanish. The following day out walking his dog a large ball of what looked like fluorescent brain matter hurtled towards them and shone a beam of light on the dog and man. Minutes later two gate-keepers of a factory in Gravesend Kent had the identical experience.

Mario Luisi Cumbria 1982. Encountered a landed small craft in a field by a weir and saw "a man and woman beside it". One held what looked like a torch which disintegrated the torch he was holding; they spoke briefly to him before taking off in the craft.

Rae Fountain who a few days before my own encounter with a landed UFO on the 17th July 1955 was abducted into an identical craft losing several hours. He had further such experiences in Edinburgh and Dover, Kent over a period of years. His was an extraordinary case history.

Eileen Clarke who was putting clothes on her washing line when a craft swooped, knocking her down to the ground, where she looked up and saw two beings in it looking down at her, it did not make a sound, neither did it have any down draft. This happened on the 26th July 1978 at Barnehurst, Kent. An identical experience, craft and humanoids seen by a lady in Bearstead, Kent in 1976. Eileen reminded me of Irene Williams, a very outgoing happy lady always joking and so happily married to Douglas Clarke who was my fellow UFO colleague in Kent, I was so sad when this meticulously careful researcher just suddenly died in 1980.

Jean Hingley of Dudley, Worcestershire. The most extraordinary of all who entertained little Space people who came down on her small back lawn and entered her house in 1980. There was much physical evidence for this extraordinary rare happening. Jean was jack blunt, uneducated, had racial prejudices, and could be so aggravating, but also totally honest with a saving sense of humour which made her so likeable. Jean later became my friend, and all of us Ufologists who met and got to know her, believed it really happened. She too died suddenly of pancreas failure not long after, was this something to do with her getting too close to the little humanoids?

Mrs. Freda Smith's neighbour who walked into a jelly-mould shaped UFO which was squatting on the lawn of Marlborough Park, Sidcup behind their houses. This was seen by all the neighbours who crowded into Mrs Smith's house when they invited me to listen to what they were experiencing in 1982. UFOS had also landed in the school playgrounds of Sidcup and the children who saw them were present at this meeting. The neighbour died shortly after going into the UFO, but he was already a sick man with a chronic complaint, he refused to tell anyone just why he did it, and what took place.

The teenage boys Martin Norris, Steve and Anthony Williams and their cousin Stewart Brown who on the 21st July 1978 were collectively abducted into a UFO at Sutton-at Hone a country area in Kent for several hours. They too were very lucky, in so far as their parents, older brothers and sisters and family all believed and supported them., as the boys at the time, did not realise they had been missing so many hours, they only remembered running towards their car when this UFO bounded across a field towards them. Now so many years later I would like to contact them and wonder what their views are now and if they gradually recalled what happened to them.

Then again back to Ellen Howson. Why do UFOS and aliens seem to time and again just tab one family and all its members? For Ellen's husband was a park keeper at Greenwich Park and Observatory where the Meridian line centre is. One morning in 1978 all the park keepers surrounded a large landed craft on the lawns. The Observatory people joined them and later the Police. It sat silent and still on the lawn for ages, when it left they were all called into the Offices and told if they ever talked of this, they would be instantly dismissed from the London Borough of Greenwich. But why? and why do all petty officials comply with this unwarranted conspiracy, for surely if we are being contacted by other worlds all the citizens of this planet Earth have the right to know. It seems China and Russia have official UFO research and encourage people to give in their UFO reports.

I thought of Spain where I try to winter some years and from many years back to the early 1960s. Years ago in Algeciras a man called Aziz Erdinch a newspaper reporter told me of a terrifying journey he had in his outboard motor boat with a UFO buzzing him in the Straits of Gibraltar. His friend a wealthy farmer round about the same period had a UFO land on his lawn, his family and servants all stood around it for about half an hour before it flew off. This same reporter was in Canada reporting on a tour of the Queen Mother's when a UFO came down low which was seen by everyone including her, yet I do not recall this going into the British newspapers.

Yes, from a UFO researcher's point of view I have been very lucky getting well over a thousand people contact me over the years both in England, Wales, Scotland, Ireland and Spain. People who know little about the subject or have shuttered minds will think I have been naive in believing the dozens and dozens of people who have come to Alan Hilton and myself over the years for help in coming to terms with their experiences. When these people come from all walks of life, some highly educated and intelligent and others semi-literate, when they are reporting all this from every country in the world, why should we who have not had these frightening experiences dismiss them? To me that displays a very arrogant, closed mind, and largely due to ignorance as these critics and cynics do not bother to study the subject before they pronounce their self-righteous views, such as Patrick Moore who has a vast knowledge about stars and what we know of the Universes to date, but absolutely nothing about UFOS because he ignores the subject.

Rae Fountain (Pseudonym)

This strange case came to light after I placed an advert, for Contact (UK) in a shop window in Lewisham, London, in the summer of 1978, for I subsequently received a telephone call from a rather nervous-sounding person who wanted to know if he could talk to me about some experiences he had had years previously, and which still troubled him. He had told nobody, he said, as people would think him a lunatic! But the advert, he had seen said no-one would deride or disbelieve if he proved to be genuine, There then followed two or three phone calls from his place of work, until it was finally arranged that he should come down to my house in Kent one evening after leaving work.

On the 12th August 1978, at about 8.30pm a taxi stopped outside my house and a man about 34 years of age with close-cut, straight dark hair and in painfully neat, new clothes was on the doorstep. This man - Rae Fountain - entered the house and after a few introductory sentences sat down and plunged into an extraordinary narration. In relating the following it was as though a door had burst within him and he was finally getting it all off his chest, something he had previously been unable to do, due to his complete ignorance of the existence of UFO organisations. This then, is Rae Fountain's story:

"This happened a very long time ago when I was nine, but it will stay in my memory forever. It was the 30th June 1955, about 3.30pm I was supposed to be going to play football at my school after school hours. This took place in a village near Leighton Buzzard (Bedfordshire) and I was loitering down a small mud track in a country lane. There were hawthorn and other bushes on either side of this road, and I was idly scuffing the ground with my boots when I noticed footprints quite close together in the mud, so I tried to put my foot in them and was tripping over as they were so close together. I then looked ahead and saw two men dressed in one-piece overalls. I could only see them from the back and would not have bothered about them except for their odd behaviour. They had small foot-strides and also they were stopping all the time and picking up earth, pebbles, leaves and weeds and placing them into something in front of them which I could not see. I started stalking them, the way children do by hiding behind bushes. Then suddenly a 'thing' just swished down across the path in front of them; it was a bluish-tinged metallic grey, roughly bell-shaped craft. This hovered a few feet off the ground.

"A door in the top half slid open; there was a protruding rim just before the rounding top on which a man could stand. A sort of concertinaing ladder came down and the two men climbed up this into the craft, the door closed, then the craft went straight up and across and swept into the sky."

I asked Rae if he could see into the craft. "Yes, I could; there was someone in there at some sort of a wheel or instrument." Then he said, "You know, it is funny, I said the colour was blue metallic grey; in fact it was like that, the way we would describe it, but in reality it was like no colour of anything I have ever seen on this earth." I asked what the underside of the craft looked like. "It was absolutely flat, but when it rose a bit as it was leaving, I could see ball-like wheels with dark, raised bands across the middle."

I exclaimed that I, too, had seen such a craft barely feet from me on the 17th July 1955. I felt Rae was telling me the truth because of these minor points in his description of the craft, which must surely have been one and the same that I saw 17 days later. Rae then said with relief, "Then you know I am telling you the truth - that I am not a nut."

"There is one point," I said. "I am struck by the fact that you described the man as having closely cropped hair; have you heard of Cedric Allingham?"

He displayed a bit of interest and said, "Is he a member of your Club? Would I be able to see him and talk to him?"

I explained that this man published a book in 1954 about a similar meeting he had had at Lossiemouth, Scotland on the 18th February 1954 with a man who indicated he had come from Mars. I said to Rae, "This is the only other description I have seen of a spaceman having closely cropped, dark brown hair. The craft was also the same as you described and which I saw, too."

I then brought the book for Rae to see and he got very excited over the picture of the craft saying, "Yes, yes, this was exactly what I saw. You said Lossiemouth, Scotland. I was on holiday on the 27th April 1975, I think, and I was walking in the hills above Holyrood Palace (Edinburgh). I love walking. I go for long walks and like being alone. I am rather an introverted being. I was walking on the hills near Arthur's Seat and there was no one there at all. I was sitting on a ridge looking down onto the hills below when I saw three craft coming down together and hovering on a flattish plateau below. They were exactly like the one I saw when I was a boy. I suppose you will think I am putting this on, but I did come here to get all this off my chest. So I assure you it did happen and again another time. This time one of these craft, the one in the centre, came up to where I was sitting and it hovered about 30 feet above my head. I just thought, 'you had your tabs on me before, now let's see what you think now I am grown up! It let a rod with a head like a loud speaker on the end down and this thing just moved down and sideways as I moved an arm or leg. It seemed to be some kind of photographing device. The rod then retracted up and the craft started spinning and flew up a bit and then it went down towards the other two craft. Then they flew off in formation towards the sea.

Before continuing with this narration, I should like to go back to the 30th June, 1955, when Rae was 9 years old, to when he saw the bell-shaped craft leaving ... the next thing Rae recalled was his Headmaster shaking him, and a number of teachers and pupils looking down at him as he lay on the ground at the side of the mud-lane. They had all been out looking for him, and the Headmaster was telling him off. He was taken back to the school and put to bed, but the following morning the Headmaster sent for him and told him they had wasted a lot of their time, he had caused a lot of anxiety, as he had been missing past night-fall, and why had he been so irresponsible and naughty? Rae did try to explain what he had seen, but was brushed aside and told he had had a bad dream. He told me that was when he became a loner. He wanted someone to explain and help him, and he knew even as a child, no one could. He knew he had not fallen asleep on the road, and yet he could not account for so much time lost.

"The next occasion was on the 14th August, 1974 at Dover, Kent. I was working in an hotel at Dover. I told you I liked walking. I used to go for long walks on the cliffs in the evenings when I was off duty. I seldom saw many people there. This time there were no people about that I noticed. I was looking out to sea when I saw three craft hovering in the distance. This time I felt afraid. I went down a cliff pathway and hid behind some boulders, peeping out on them at the same time. They gradually came in from the sea and one landed or hovered just above the sand on the beach below me and the other one came and hovered over it. They were exactly like the previous craft I had seen, metallic-grey and bell-shaped. The central one, which somewhat resembled an elongated football, landed right on the edge of the cliff. If you have not been to Dover, the edges of the cliffs curve one after the other and this was on the curve of one of these edges, so that I had a side-angle view. I was surprised it (the UFO) was not the same shape as the other two. This really looked like a football. It was standing on three tripod legs and there was a door open with the same concertineering (sic) ladder. Suddenly two people 'in all enveloping silvery-white suits came down the ladder. I pressed back, afraid, as they started to come down the cliff pathway. They were talking loudly."

I asked if they passed the rocks he was hiding behind. "Yes," he said. Did they see him? "I don't know. They appeared not to. They were talking to each other all the time. Their heads were completely covered by a whitish head covering with a visor over the eyes. They passed down the path. One had a shining receptacle in his hand. One appeared much slighter and shorter - I thought it must be woman."

"Why did you think the other person was a woman? Could you see any shape?" "No, the garments were loose - similar to what an American astronaut wears; not quite so bulging, but you could not distinguish the shape of them exactly. They went down towards the two craft hovering over the beach, but when they went down there was a small pool in the rocks below, where they stopped. They sucked up some water through a tube, then they looked for a few moments at the smaller craft."

When asked about the craft's size, he answered, "I'd say about 35ft, the same as on the other occasions, but the big one on the cliff was longer. They then turned round and started to walk back up the path. I felt very afraid and pushed well back. As they started climbing up the cliff path they were talking loudly all the time in their own language. I couldn't resist peeping as they came nearer. All I noticed was the eyes; the visors over their eyes must have enlarged them because I could see them distinctly. They had two pupils - one was still and the other appeared to be moving."

"Are you sure you saw this? They must have been a few feet from you."

"Yes, I know. I don't know why, because I've thought of this since, but I could see the eyes distinctly as they walked past me. The pupils were deep mauve and the part where we have white seemed green."

I commented "My God! Surely you were scared?"

"Yes, I was. I shrank back but at the same time I felt compelled to look. They did not seem to see me at all, they just passed on up to the top of the cliff Then I next saw them going up the ladder. I then pressed back again. Then the two craft on the beach rose and flew backwards to the sea. The larger one joined them and took up the same position in the centre, then they flew backwards in formation until they disappeared."

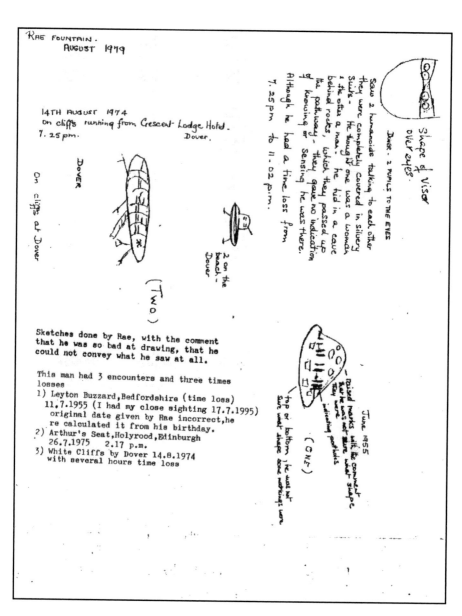

RAE FOUNTAIN.
AUGUST 1979

14TH AUGUST 1974
On cliffs running from Crescent Lodge Hotel.
7.25 pm.   Dover.

DOVER

On cliffs at Dover

Shape of Visor over eyes.
DOVER - 2 PUPILS TO THE EYES

Saw 2 humanoids talking to each other
they were completely covered in silvery
suits. He thought one was a woman
1 the other a man. He hid in a cave
behind rocks, which they passed up
the pathway - they gave no indication
of knowing or sensing he was there.
Although he had a time loss from
7.25 pm to 11.02 p.m.

(Two)

2 on the
beach. -
Dover

Sketches done by Rae, with the comment
that he was so bad at drawing, that he
could not convey what he saw at all.

This man had 3 encounters and three times
losses
1) Leyton Buzzard,Bedfordshire (time loss)
   11.7.1955 (I had my close sighting 17.7.1995)
   original date given by Rae incorrect,he
   re calculated it from his birthday.
2) Arthur's Seat,Holyrood,Edinburgh
   26.7.1975   2.17 p.m.
3) White Cliffs by Dover 14.8.1974
   with several hours time loss

June 1955

(ONE)

- Raised marks with the comment
he/she was not sure what shape
they were
infecting portholts

- top or bottom ; he was not
sure what shape some markings were

Sketches by Rae Fountain

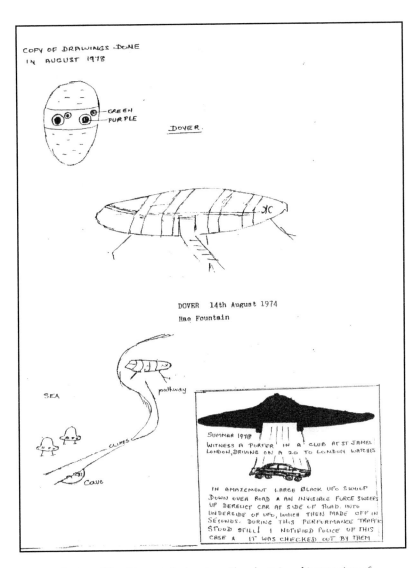

Copies of Rae Fountain's drawings (for clarity) and impression of
his Colleague's sighting in Kent on 16th July 1978

While narrating this, Rae appeared to be reliving most of the experiences and scarcely noticed me. The few questions I asked were hurriedly replied to as he went on to recall what he had seen. However, he now seemed to come back to me and a bit nervously said: "I don't think I am the only one who has had these weird experiences. I have a friend at work who on the 16th July this year (1978) was motoring from the Kent coast in the evening on the A20. About 9.00pm he was passing Farningham when a large dark craft swept down across the road. He was on the slow lane at the time and on the grass verge just ahead of him to the left was a derelict, abandoned car. Time seemed to stand still, he said, and all traffic sounds stopped. A terrific but invisible force seemed to paralyse not only him but also the car. This force lifted the derelict car horizontally into the air before his disbelieving eyes. It just scooped it, evenly and not-too-fast, up into the under-side of the craft, then something seemed to shut and it zoomed off This man went back to the same spot a few days later with a friend to examine the grass verge. He found the markings of the car and realised he had not imagined it at all and that it had happened."

This made me sit up in my chair, for unknown to Rae Fountain a Mrs. Daphne Thomas of Thamesmead had rung me a few weeks earlier to say she had read a little about me in the "Kentish Times". She hesitatingly told me she didn't really believe in UFOs, but on the 16th July 1978 she and her husband had been motoring up from the coast. It was a fine day with a blue and cloudless sky, and she had been idly watching a craft following the lines of the motorway. It was quite high up in the sky and was glowing orange with the last rays of the sun. A continuous orange flame shot out from the rear of the craft. She pointed it out to her husband. He had to watch the traffic, but when the opportunity arose he stole a second or so's glance and said he thought it was a jet. This went on for about 50 miles and after watching it intensely she said: "It can't be a jet, the flame at the back stays the same short length. It's cigar-shaped and is leaving no vapour trail. Perhaps it's a UFO!" So he glanced up every so often and said she might be right. At about 9.05pm (it was now twilight) they reached a known spot on the A20 at Farningham where the craft suddenly disappeared!

Oddly enough, a Mr Titler (ex-RAF) and his wife were returning to their home in Farningham at 2.00am on the 5th March 1978 when at the same spot on the A20 they saw a brilliantly lit, turquoise cigar-shaped craft with some type of cockpit at the front. It rapidly crossed the road and passed across the fields and open countryside. (There might be some significance to the theory that a UFO may be seen by different people perhaps months or years later in the same spot)

With regard to the abduction of the derelict car by the UFO, I reported this incident to my local police station, and they appeared to be more than casually interested... (1 take reports of all UFO sightings within my area to the local police.) On this occasion they asked me numerous questions and I had the impression that they keep a list of all abandoned cars within their territory, and that they had noted this car had gone.

Rae said once the craft moved off, his friend returned to normal and could hear other traffic. His limbs were trembling so violently he did not know how he drove the rest of the way to Pall Mall, London where he worked. He felt if that was what they could do to an empty car, what would they do with him if he had lingered.

I knew Rae could not possibly know about Mrs Daphne Thomas or Mr Titler, so improbable as it seemed to me at the time, this derelict car business must have been true, so too should I reasonably suppose were his own experiences.

Rae had promised to contact me again shortly, but he failed to do this, thinking he needed more help I enlisted my friend Timothy Good to try and trace him. We both went to his work place, and were told he had worked there but now left. Then quite by chance a year later Dave and Rose Chatterton found Rae living at a S. E. London address. He had apparently gone to live and work in Scotland and married there. Then he and his wife came down South. Unfortunately the first recession had started, and he was without work or accommodation when we met again, and was temporarily with relatives. Despite their worrying circumstances they agreed to come over to the Chatterton's home one evening and Rae re-related his story. His wife was staggered, he had never told her any of this, and UFOs were something that had never entered her thinking before. Then she reflected and said she knew and trusted her husband, so no matter how unbelievable, she knew those things must have happened to him. To her credit, Rae was a changed being, happy, hopeful he would have a job and Council house shortly - quite different from the nervous introverted being I had met the year before.

The abridged account was published by Dan Goring Editor of Earthlink (Winter 1979) so I should add a point he left out. On the 30th June 1955 when Rae saw the craft leaving he fell asleep at the side of the lane. By 9.00p.m the Headmaster and teachers were all out looking for him and eventually found him there, he got a good shaking and scolding and was sent to bed. The following morning he was called to the Headmaster's office, and asked to explain his absence. Rae did try to, he was roundly told not to fabricate rubbish, so thereafter he decided he would never mention this to anyone, including his family again. All through his growing up years he had repeated and vivid nightmares of having been taken into that craft spanning the road, being subjected to painful and horrible examinations. I did ascertain the point that he had seen the craft leaving and then fell asleep. "That was correct", he said. Rather puzzled, I asked if he knew what time the craft left, he said he did not know, it was still light anyway, he knew the time he first saw the men, as he was supposed to be on his way to play football. The longest day of the year is the 21st June, so it must have turned dark only after 10 pm.

On the 27th April 1975 when Rae was sitting on Arthur's Seat and the three craft landed on the hills below, Dave Chatterton was unable to accept that in this very popular tourist area, no other people were about, he raised the point quite accusingly. Far from looking ruffled, I noted Rae's expression, he then looked puzzled himself and said "Yes you are right, I had not thought about it, but there were no people there at all during the duration, and come to think of it everything was very quiet, no sounds at all anywhere." In 1978 none of the people present had read of these points raised now in every Abduction book, although Timothy Good had been in America and interviewed people who felt they had been abducted. Tim being a musician checked that a concert had been given by Leonard Bernstein with the London Symphony Orchestra, Rae had said he had gone to Edinburgh especially to attend this.

In fact I have a thick folder of this case, the points we raised and the checks we made were pretty thorough and consistent with the knowledge we had in 1978. Today, individuals, organisations and small groups are amalgamating far more to pool their knowledge, not only Britain, but worldwide, there is a growing awareness that we in the Ufology world have to pull together to achieve anything. Over the years I have done everything one individual can to promote this.

An observation I made then despite having talked to so many people with similar stories to tell, is that though Dave Chatterton felt disbelief, both Rose and I reacted in the same way. Fortunately for the witness we had had similar experiences of Time and Dimension distortion when in close proximity to a UFO - your sole reaction is of helpless lameness. How can you satisfactorily explain an incident to someone when you know all the while they are emphatically disbelieving you, at the same time you are feeling slightly incredulous yourself, although you are positive it happened! Can the power that motivates a UFO when you are within certain circumference of it affect your brain wave patterns? This feeling of puzzle and wonder increased when I went up to Scotland in November 1979. A warm sunny day, we took a special trip to Arthur's Seat with a cine-camera. I looked into the vicinity below and wondered how Rae Fountain had seen 3 craft, 35ft. in diameter fit into the hollow of relatively small hills below Arthur's Seat?

How had I seen a 100ft craft fit into the narrow lower Greenwich Road in 1976, and how had Rose in 1971 seen a UFO in a small alleyway at the bottom of her small garden, enlarge as it came up and hover over her, covering the whole width of it. Ditto too why do people time and again tell me in great detail, the colour and shape of a humanoids eyes, when they might have been yards from them?

Here the sceptics will no doubt in triumph exclaim that this is because it is an hallucination in the first place. Isn't it time we accepted with the weight of evidence Ufologists world-wide have collected, that Alien technology is beyond our knowledge and comprehension.

NOTE: When interviewed the second time Rae thought his date of 30th June 1955 was incorrect calculating it from his birthday, he decided it was the 11th July 1955.

Investigators – Whilst Timothy Good and Dave Chatterton disbelieved this man, Margaret Fry and Rose Chatterton felt he was genuine.

Sutton-at-Hone. Kent. Saturday 21st July 1978 10.00p.m. to 2.30a.m.

Simon aged 21 years, Anthony 14 years and Mark 24 years were talking at the Williams' gate in Barnehurst, Kent. They were waiting for Stephen (16) and Stuart (16) to return from the cinema.

It was a warm clear summer's evening, as they stood chatting. Suddenly they noticed a very bright star, the only one in the light blue sky. It was 9.00 p.m. when this star came down and down, and then they realised it was a strange craft in the shape of a large Mexican hat as they described it. It had a red light at the top of the dome (see illustrations) and was flashing red, blue, yellow and green lights around the lower rim. It seemed to be revolving, at the same time flying across the sky fairly slowly, and then this rapidly went away into the distance.

Feeling terribly excited about this, as soon as the other boys returned, they told them and were all for driving out into the Kent countryside to see if they could see anything further. The two boys didn't believe them, but said "O.K. we'll ask Mum". Mrs. Williams agreed with reservation "you can go, but don't stay out too late, and keep Anthony up". She had a large family, Anthony being the youngest.

The boys piled into the one car belonging to their friend Martin. The nearest bit of open countryside to them was at Sutton-at-Hone a half-hour's drive away. When they arrived by open fields, they parked the car at the side of the road at 10.00p.m. Some electric pylons were some distance away in the fields. After sky watching for a half-hour, they were disappointed, and headed towards the car. It was then they noticed a huge star like white light hovering alongside the electric pylon, this then turned to an oval shape, with a pointed front, that now came across the field towards them! They took fright and ran. This they said was the size of a Cortina car. At this point Anthony and Stephen stopped and hesitated, then went a few steps back. Then they again saw the Mexican hat revolving near to ground level across the fields. As the brothers stood watching this

77

craft, Simon, whom they said had been the most afraid had already reached the car. Anthony then ran to Stuart and Martin, and they all decided they would go up a hillock to see if they could still see the Mexican hat, but trees obscured their view. At this they all started to feel afraid again, and raced down to join Simon who was already in the car, when they piled in, they could not get home fast enough.

On reaching home, they found Mrs. Williams anxiously standing at the gate, she told me she was about to tell them off roundly, when she saw how tired they all looked, and also afraid. They told her what they had seen, and she immediately made them all go to bed, Simon had to be got up very early anyway to join his ship at Gravesend in the morning, he was in the Merchant Navy. He was her nephew. As soon as the boys arrived Mrs Williams had checked her watch, it was 3.00a.m. In the morning she asked her adult sons and their wives to come over, they had a family discussion. After that they decided to ask me to call over. They either got my name from the Police or Library, or they may have seen something in the Kentish Times I forget which. The Kentish Times did print a few of the hundreds of UFO reports I had in 1978, a North Kent flap year.

When I arrived at the Williams house, the boys had been encouraged to go out for the evening. All the family met me. They related the above to mc and then expressed their anxiety that something had happened to the boys, which they seemed totally unaware of. They had lost about three and a half hours the night before. When they had gone to bed they were all too tired to note the time except of course Mrs. Williams who had been anxiously watching the clock. Could I explain what had happened?

I am afraid at that time I only vaguely felt they may have been abducted into one of the craft they had seen, and maybe their memory of it had been blotted out. I had no idea at the time that people could have their memories retrieved with hypnosis. In any case I thought this was a hospital medical treatment, and if undertaken privately would cost too much.

However, they certainly would not have wanted the boys to undergo any such treatment, their anxiety stemmed from 'would this have some adverse effect on their health?' On this point I was able to reassure them. To the best of my knowledge, no one had suffered any ill effects from seeing UFOs, abductions I knew nothing about. Or should I say the abduction scenario we are now getting fairly frequently.

Somewhat reassured, the Williams' agreed I could interview the boys on their arrival, providing I did not make them aware of the missing time factor. Simon, their cousin, had already left for his Merchant Naval ship in the early morning, before the boys awoke, so it was not till some months after when he returned home from one of his voyages, that I was able to interview him before he had the chance to discuss things with the boys. This was arranged with the cooperation of the family, so that his witness account was quite independent.

Stuart who was a friend who lived in the North, had to leave on the Sunday morning, so that his account was also given separately from the rest of the boys. The two brothers and Martin would have obviously discussed the night's happenings on the Sunday afternoon, before meeting me. All the boys' reports were consistent. Again it had not occurred to Martin who was older that they had missed time. I think they all assumed it was about 11.30p.m. when they had gone straight to bed.

My interview with Martin took place as he was getting ready to return to his home in Sittingbourne, where he lived with his Mother, they had all only been visiting for the weekend. I made him promise to contact me, if he ever saw anything again.

On the 27th August 1978 it was a lovely warm clear evening and Capella was particularly low and bright, with numerous other stars out twinkling brightly. I went on to the porch with my binoculars. It was then I saw a small star, looping the loop, seemingly in and out of the stars! I called my husband and he and I tried to focus on this object with the binoculars, but it was far too fast. I was so taken with the antics of this small star. Sometimes when it approached another star it seemed to flare up. This went on quite a while, when the phone rang, I was reluctant to answer it, but thought I would look through the windows. It was Martin, he said I would never believe him, seeing this was the second time, and he would not have rung, except that his Mum was with him and watching this too, she would speak to me. I assured him Ron and I were watching it also. I would talk to him later. Then I went back to the porch, Ron said it had just zoomed off.

I then held a discussion with the Norris's who said they had watched the star loop the loop like in one of those 'Walt Disney's films'. That was exactly how it had looked. The object must have been miles up in the atmosphere to have been seen simultaneously in Bexleyheath and Sittingbourne on the Kent coast, and to appear to be weaving in and out of the stars. It must have been enormous for us to see it with the naked eye at all, and what sort of technology could make a thing of that size manoeuvre about so? Imagine Concorde looping the loop with hundreds of air passengers! I have the assurance of air pilots that we simply haven't the technology for all these capers.

Bluestone Walk, Warley. Worcestershire - 4th January 1979 - 6.45a.m. to 7.30a.m

A number of people have written second-hand accounts of this extraordinary happening usually somewhat inaccurately. They did not get to know Jean Hingley, I did, and I still have her tapes asking me to tell people what she felt and thought, the only other people who knew her as well were Eileen Morris who now lives in Canada and befriended her, and one of my fellow investigators Phyllis Mooney who also extended her understanding and friendship.

The Daily Mirror and other national newspapers had carried the story of how Beings with 3ft wingspan had flown through the kitchen window - or they ate mince pies! I though this surely is all totally inaccurate, so I wrote to Jean on the 15th January 1979 and to my surprise she replied on the 24th January. She said she had shoals of letters, and had picked mine out as the most sensible of the lot, and God knows she needed someone who would believe her, but also have some common sense! I have only a couple of letters from Jean, she did not like having to write, but from thereon she phoned almost daily, sometimes she would be on the phone for hours. A short while after I first contacted Jean, Eileen Morris who lived near by visited Jean. Eileen had for years taken an interest in UFOs and initially went to see if she could find out more about the subject. She got more than she bargained for! As Jean took a liking to her, Eileen had to take on the role of acting a buffer between Jean and other people. Eileen was, right into her 90's, an extremely perceptive, sensitive person. She had little in common with Jean who was forthright, full of humour and prejudices which made one want to shake her at times, then this saving grace of humour would come to the fore. Jean was also totally honest and naïve, she would never ever have invented or imagined such a story as hers. She had a sharp wit, was intelligent with a good deal of down-to-earth common sense with it, but little or no education. Not many people could have put a fast one over Jean, her very background had seen to that. She was born in London, her parents died when she was young, and she was shifted to the West Midlands where she was fostered about from one set of foster parents to another. Jean could read and write, but did not like doing much of either, even after her experience. She did not want to read UFO books or hear of other people's sightings or close encounters.

I have read that Jean was supposed to be troubled with religious doubts, that is rubbish. She had a simple, unquestioning faith in God. She told me she had not been to Church for a while as she did not like the music they were playing nowadays. That had nothing to do with religious doubts, Jean was just a very simple straightforward person. She liked the factory where she worked, because they could have a laugh and she could earn money to give them a comfortable living. Her husband was the first person she could really call her own in her life and she adored him, they were very happily

80

married. They had no children, but she wasted no time on regrets, they fostered children from time to time, and housed abandoned animals, they led full lives.

All Jean's interests were purely limited to her domestic environment, she only took an interest in 'Home politics' expressing strong insular views, abroad could have been the Moon to Jean, she was totally intolerant and prejudiced about blacks, foreigners living in our country ... the usual intolerant prejudices people have when they do not read, travel or think. They alienated Eileen and myself, but suddenly she would be quite humble - saying she did not know much, or 'what the hell, let's have a laugh'. That was my friend Jean, a very likeable person, despite her faults, but then haven't we all got them? The one thing Jean took very seriously to her dying day was the Incident.

In the early hours of the 4th January 1979 it was dark, freezing, with thick snow and ice everywhere, one of the worst British winters on record this century. It would take anything from half an hour to an hour for people to de-ice their cars and get them going; it was impossible to clear pathways. These are facts that are conveniently overlooked when people like Albert Budden expound their theories on the Hingley case. The houses on this Council Estate were all linked, with very tiny gardens, their back lawn was only 17ft by 11ft, and there was a carport at the end of this, then an alleyway.

Cyril, Jean's husband went out of the house between 5.00a.m. and 5.15a.m. to attend to his car to go to work at the Cement Works near by, there was a door by the carport that led to a back road from their house. Jean worked in a factory some miles away near Birmingham, making sound proofing for cars, she did not have to catch a bus till much later, although she was in the habit of wearing her dressing gown to get up to prepare sandwiches for her husband to take with him.

They had lived in this Council house 9 years, it was small with two bedrooms, and on a small estate near the open countryside, with a quarry nearby, this was on the edge of the village of Rowley Regis, near Warley in Worcestershire. The whole estate was surrounded by wasteland. Jean stood at the kitchen door and waved Cyril off to work, and then through the window she noticed a light. Talking to their Alsatian 'Hobo' she said, "Master has left the car port light on" so they went into the garden to turn it off. Then she saw that the light was from an 'orange ball' low in the sky. She assumed this was the rising sun and went in doors, leaving the side door open for the dog which was still sniffing about the lawn, it then came in and moments later she heard a sound "zee ... zee ... zee" and three little Beings floated past her through the open floor. They were slender, small and glowed with a brilliant light, they glided about a foot off the floor towards the Hall and Living Room. Jean was terrified and clutched the kitchen sink behind her, speechless, she felt all her blood draining down to her feet. Hobo was hobbling towards its drinking bowl, swaying from side to side, its hair sticking out all over its body like a hedgehog's, it seemed drugged and just flopped down, stretching out stiff on the floor, with its eyes staring fixedly. Usually this huge Alsatian was not afraid of anything, being of such an uncertain breed people were afraid of him!

Jean also felt paralysed, her mouth was open, her jaw ached, and she kept feeling the blood steeping through to her toes, after awhile this sensation went and she FLOATED a foot off the floor. The kitchen door was still open, but she now felt warm, she floated towards the Living Room door (she weighed 13 stone). With mouth still open, she watched these three little creatures by the Christmas tree, they were chattering and shaking it, trying to topple the fairy doll on top. The light around them was so brilliant she had to shield her eyes; they seemed able to control this as they dimmed it, and she could now see them clearly. They were about 3ft 6 inches tall, had greyish white complexions, brilliant diamond jet black eyes which seemed sunk in the sockets, their mouths were just a thin line, their hands and feet were pointed, but this may have been because they were encased completely in a green/silver tunic and trousers. There were six buttons in pairs down their chests. They had wings, these were transparent and shimmered the most beautiful colours, and she could not tell if these were mechanical or part of them, but they were iridescent and lovely and they floated about the Living Room touching everything. Christmas cards, the clock, radio, furniture and a newspaper on the table with a picture of the Queen, thin bands of silver streamers floated away from their shoulders. She noticed when one Being floated horizontally over the dining table, these streamers stayed in line with his body, two of these were thicker and he seemed able to control them as feelers. When sitting in the room the wings folded back in pleats.

At last Jean managed to speak "Three of you, and one of me, what are you going to do, what do you want of me?" Each put their hands to the operating buttons on their chests, and then metallic voices said in unison "we come from the sky", at no time during the hour they were there did they speak through their mouths and at times Jean wondered if they were some form of robot, as they had no expressions on their faces either. The voices that came out were in English. Looking at the picture of the Queen, she said "That is our Queen" but they did not understand, so she asked if they also had a Leader, they said yes, they had a leader, and she said the Queen was ours, and why had they not gone to her, she was a Lady, They said "You are a Lady". In her naive way Jean chatted on about this being a man's world, and women had to do all the work here. She told them about her job, and she said they seemed very fascinated about that. She told them about children, which seemed to particularly interest them, and animals she had taken on. When she asked them about themselves they were not so forthcoming. They did tell her their planet was cold and they did not have fire or electricity. I was particularly interested in this as at the time I was reading the book of T. C. Lethbridge

The Legend of the Sons of God (Routledge & Kegan Paul – London), in which he says a French expedition had gone to Easter Island in the Pacific and the wife of the leader Francis Maziere a Polynesian herself, was able to record for the anthropologists there, the legends of the Islanders. It is worth recording -

a) The inhabitants of Jupiter have settled the concordance of the planets
b) The first planet that man will reach will be Venus
c) Our bodies cannot stand more than two months on other planets
d) All the planets worship the Sun
e) Not many stars are inhabited
f) Amongst us are people whom we cannot see
g) The current and light of Venus are produced by the air
h) Two planets, Jupiter and Mars have no electricity, there are no winds, and they are like the earth
i) Only our earth has men of different colours
j) There are people living on the Moon

At one stage Jean told them they put up a Christmas tree to celebrate the birth of Jesus, and he was born then - they said they knew all about Jesus. When they looked at the Sunday paper, she noticed the Honours List, and said, "Those people have been made Lords", they said "There in only one Lord". Frequently they increased the light in the centre of the 'fish bowls' over their heads, this would hurt Jean's eyes, and she would tell them so, when they would again diminish them.

There was a corner unit couch in the room on which they were sitting, when they got excited about something Jean said, they bounced up and down like children. "Be careful of my furniture," she said sharply, so they put the light up! She felt she had better be careful of what she said, as though small, she felt they had the power to harm her. On a whole though, throughout the visitation Jean felt very warm and happy with them. She told them she could not call them creatures, so she would say 'gentlemen'. Thinking of Bruce Forsyth she said 'Nice to see you, nice', they repeated 'Nice'. It seems to me these alien Beings when they do communicate, which doesn't seem to be very often, tell people what they want to know and believe, and they keep to the level of their knowledge and intelligence. For example Jean even elected to tell them people should live in their own countries, and they agreed that she was right.

When they floated about the room their wings fluttered gently, and when they went into the Hall, the wings folded back in pleats, they circled the hall then floated upstairs, then down again, they picked up the tapes (which never functioned again). They looked at the drinks left over from a Christmas party, which were on the sideboard, and then she asked if they would like a drink 'Water' they said. So Jean floated into the kitchen to fetch water and four glasses, one for herself to drink to show them water was harmless and not poisoned. As she got near to them, she could hardly hold the tray, they seemed to magnetise it towards them. Each picked up a glass as she did, "they seemed about to lift their bowls, when they saw me watching them they put the power light on, so that I did not actually see them drink, when they put the light down, the water had gone".

They told her they had been to Australia, New Zealand and America 'we come down here to try to talk to people, but they don't seem to be interested'. 'Shall I tell people on Earth about you? They said 'Yes, we have been here before and we shall come again.' They also told her everyone will go to heaven, and there are beautiful colours there.

Jean decided to fetch them mince pies on a plate, she took six, as she thought it was rude to only put three, in case one of them wanted more. She always talks of their hands being magnetised, even their feet. She saw them looking at cigarettes, she offered them one, when they refused, she offered them Cyril's cigars! Then she thought she would show them how to use them, so lit a match, at this they leapt back as though in fright, and immediately began to float towards the back door. She stubbed out the cigarette and called 'Come back, come back! She floated after them, as they went into the back yard she saw the orange glowing 'thing' sitting on the lawn. It was small, ten feet long by about 4 ft high. It had round portholes, and seemed to be covered with some sort of shiny plastic; there was something that reminded her of a scorpion's tail at the back, and a sort of wheel on the top.

The mince pies were still magnetised to their pointed hands, as they entered this. It was dark inside. She called after them 'you could at least thank me for the water and mince pies'. At that the door slid shut and the small object went up, just past the street light at the back road, it let out a blue thin beam with sparks at the end, like a flue brush, the old fashioned ones they used for chimneys, with that they flashed their lights twice, she felt they were saying good-bye and thank you.

I am sure the more sophisticated amongst you readers will think what a load of old rubbish, if they are such advanced Beings why do they have to hold such inane pointless conversations. If they are here to observe, they were doing just that, equating to the level of her understanding.

You may recall, if familiar with UFO lore, Dr. Daniel Fry PhD engineering executive, a prime mover in liquid fuelled missile programming, also a lecturer and world traveler, on the 4th July 1950 was taken into a Spacecraft, and was imparted information of the type few ordinary people would grasp. Yet when he asked how they produced the tremendous energy necessary to accelerate to such high velocities he was told to make the explanation truly understandable, they would have to extend his knowledge considerably in the area we refer to as Physics.

After the small craft left that freezing January morning there was a deep impression where the craft had settled on the lawn. Hobo came to life and wandered around the garden sniffing at the grass and plants. Jean still felt warm and happy and went over to her neighbour's who was ill in bed. She told her about the winged Beings, 'Angels' said her neighbour 'Don't be stupid' said Jean in her common sense way 'They were no such things' 'Call the police then,' 'I'll do just that'. Jean rang the Oldbury Police, who said they would come immediately. Then she rang her husband at work, she was a bit put out as initially he just laughed and told her to go and get a hair set, and tell the girls there about it. The hairdressers were more receptive, they had known Jean for quite some years and believed her.

Prior to this the police had arrived and examined the indent on the lawn, noted the fact that all the snow had melted off her roof and that of her neighbours and their gardens and pathways. They saw a mystery ring that had developed in the glass of her kitchen door. Jean's wedding ring had turned snow white and by now the shock of the experience had set in. She looked pale and felt ill. The police decided to call a UFO Investigation Service in Birmingham, who came and measured the indent 8ft x 4ft., took soil samples for analysis - What were the results? I wonder. Did anyone run a Geiger counter or any such instrument over the material of the sofa and areas the Beings touched? Was the radio, tapes and tape recorder etc. examined, they no longer functioned after that. It seems to me if researchers concentrated along these practical lines eventually some tangible evidence will emerge, the pointers are there in quite a number of CE4 cases. Instead people, mostly arm chair researchers come up with such nimbus theories, that also conveniently overlook these factual pointers, and then everyone else jumps on the band wagon to show how open-minded and smart they are, for after all, there isn't one shred of evidence for the UFO phenomenon ... or is there?

Fortunately Jean's Doctor who knew her very well and was a sensible man, said he believed her, as he knew she would not make such a thing up, but he could not treat her beyond giving her support, as he simply did not know the cause of her physical symptoms, and therefore would do more harm than good. Jean came out in rashes and her eyes were extremely sore, she had to wear dark glasses for the best part of the year. When Jean came to me in August, she could not bear sunlight. She was also getting migraines, something she had never had before, in addition there was a raised puncture mark in the centre of her forehead, which I pointed out and she had not noticed. The moment one of her headaches came on, this would radiate a circle of purple under the skin. All these are physical symptoms we as a whole in the Ufology world, should be drawing to the attention of the medical world. There is an abysmal failure in the medical profession to know this phenomenon even exists.

Conversely over the years a large number of nurses have come to me with UFO reports, they all say they haven't the guts to talk about this in their hospitals. Well, my view is with a greater cooperation with each other and an amalgamation of groups, we can collectively do something about this.

Poor Jean like the majority of people who have this experience, had to put up with harassment from her bosses mainly, eventually she had to leave her job. She was pretty strong willed and took them to an Industrial Tribunal and after many months of upset, she eventually got some compensation and decided to make the most of her enforced leisure. She came down to Kent to stay with me with Eileen Morris, whom she felt needed a break. Eileen had just tragically lost her son. We went to London and went shopping. Jean wanted expensive presents out of her compensation for Cyril. She was warm hearted and kind, though forthright to a point of tactlessness. We went to a BUFORA UFO Conference; Jean wasn't impressed. When listening to Alan Hynek she said aloud "Come, Margaret, let's go, he's boring me to tears, I don't understand a word he is saying'. The final straw was when a French abductee tried desperately to tell her story, and was hustled out of the hall hastily. Jean said 'Rude lot! That's the type of person they should be listening to'. Going out into the foyer, I met Dr. Leo Sprinkle for the first time, we got talking. Jean and Eileen were talking elsewhere. I told Dr. Sprinkle about her and how frustrated she was that no one would listen to her. He said 'My dear Lady, lead me to her, I have crossed the Atlantic to talk to people like her'. But the BUFORA Committee gave him no chance to do any such thing.

We had arranged to meet the Essex UFO Group at this Conference, and all of them came out early, they wanted to meet Jean, so we all went to a Restaurant for the rest of the evening and had a happy laughing time. It was here that Phyllis Mooney met Jean and continued the friendship, visiting her at her home in the Midlands, she also took photos of the indent in the lawn which was still distinctly there eight months later, no grass had grown over the area. I had advised Cyril to take periodic photos of it, in addition many people wanted to take away their kitchen door. I told them on no account to let them. These things were tangible physical evidence for Jean's experience, and she should keep them there for her own benefit.

In the ensuing months of that year 1979 Jean began to feel the Space Beings were contacting her on occasions telepathically... whenever she felt they had she would phone me; she developed psychic abilities, she foresaw the death and funeral of a friend, which really distressed her. One evening Jean told me 'they' had told her to go up to the Quarry, where she would see one of their ships there. She walked almost up to it, then it took off, she said it was huge, perched on the edge of the Quarry and had an insignia on its side. I asked her to send a drawing, meaning the Craft; she sketched the emblem on a scrap of paper. Now, as I said before, Jean never read books, she used to get Cyril to read her the newspaper, so she certainly knew nothing about Ummo or the craft at San Jose de Valderas.

San Jose de Valderas	Mario Luisi (?)	Jean Hingley	Rae Fountain
ⱖ	℮ ⱴ•	JHL	ⱦ

The craft which Jean never sketched for me she said was black, a torpedo shape in sections, when I told her I too, years before had seen a UFO the bottom half of which was in sections, she wasn't in the least interested. She never asked me about it or wanted to know about anybody's UFO sightings.

My Diary for 1982 tells me that Jean and I had a long chat on the 16th July. On the 22nd July, Phyllis Mooney phoned and said, 'this is going to be a shock to you. Jean is dead'. 'How?' I asked stunned. 'She had pancreas failure, she was gone in 4 days' was the reply. This was 31 months after her incredible experience. Not only I, but also anyone who ever met and knew her had any doubt that she had it.

No amount of Albert Budden theorising about Jean having "a very real experience to her, which nevertheless all took place in her mind," caused by electrical impulses from the Quarry altering her brain wave patterns, can dispute that Jean did have the experience on a physical level. What I feel is a total flaw in the theories of Budden/Blackmore is that neither take into consideration that people from all areas of the world, and in all walks of life could not possibly have the self same mental aberrations, even by the laws of mathematics, or Sods law! This would be totally impossible. In the case of Jean Hingley and many, many others the physical evidence is there. I sincerely hope people will read my book in conjunction with Albert Budden's book.

Let me reiterate in the Hingley incident the physical evidence was there 1) All the snow melted over the house and grounds, also over the houses and grounds of her neighbours, that in sub-zero Arctic weather, witnessed by the Police less than 20 minutes later. 2) The deep indents and markings on the lawn, also witnessed by the police and numerous Ufologists. 3) The deep impression of a circle in the glass of the kitchen door. 4) The transistor radio and tapes which never worked again. 5) The raised bump in the centre of Jean's forehead, with a deep puncture mark in the centre of it, which turned deep purple, with a ring of red radiating out from it every time Jean got a bad headache 6) Jean's wedding ring which immediately turned snow white. 7) Finally, the appalling headaches which Jean never had before the incident, the very sore eyes and rashes which lasted months, and was witnessed by me and others in August of that year, eight months later.

In addition no one thought to check for any form of radiation or whatever chemical changes occur when extra-terrestrial Beings come into contact with a sofa and other objects touched. Why? Because Ufologists then did not have the awareness or expertise of such points in connection with abductions or CE4 cases in January 1979.

Neither has this situation improved much today, we now have the awareness, but not the facilities, nor yet the professionals sufficiently interested to conduct these Laboratory experiments. Yet all these practical points are conveniently overlooked by the latter day theorist Ufologists.

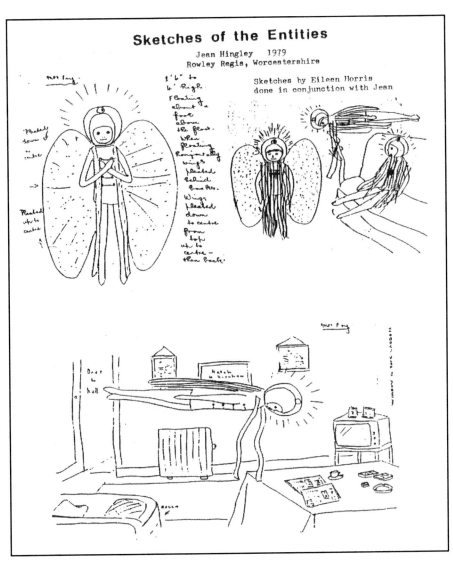

Jean Hingley's interpretation of the three 'green men' as drawn by Eileen Morris

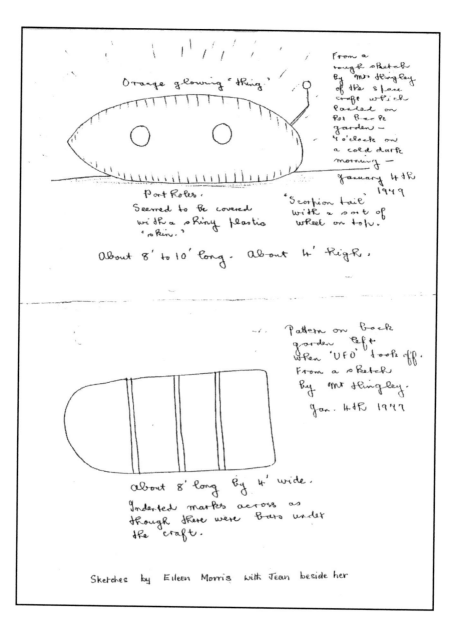

Orange glowing "thing"

From a rough sketch by Mr. Hingley of the space craft which landed on his back garden — 4 o'clock on a cold dark morning — January 4th 1979

Port Holes.
Seemed to be covered with a shiny plastic "skin."

"Scorpion tail" with a sort of wheel on top.

About 8' to 10' long. About 4' high.

Pattern on back garden left when 'UFO' took off. From a sketch by Mr. Hingley. Jan. 4th 1979

about 8' long by 4' wide.
Indented marks across as though there were bars under the craft.

Sketches by Eileen Morris with Jean beside her

Sketches of the Craft as seen by Jean Hingley

90

OLDBURY

News Telep[hone]

THURSDAY, JANUARY 11, 1979

No. 5490

Hard to believe — or is it?

With the recent "sightings" in New Zealand, UFOs are once again much in the news — and now we have reports of one in our own locality.

Mrs Jean Hingley, a perfectly sane and respectable Rowley Regis housewife claims not only to have seen a UFO but also to have met its occupants!

"Rubbish, we hear you say. Pull the other one." But can we really dismiss Mrs Hingley as just another crank, and her lurid account of her experience as a hallucination?

Her story does take some believing. Nevertheless, there are a growing number of scientists who no longer dismiss these experiences as a pure figment of the imagination.

And it is too easy to dismiss these claims. True, there are constant reports of strange lights and objects in the sky which often turn out to be flares, balloons or high flying aircraft.

Our universe contains many unexplained mysteries and though life on other planets has yet to be proved we cannot say that it does not exist.

'I met UFO men' says housewife Jean . . . .

A Rowley Regis housewife claimed this week to have had a close encounter of the third kind — contact with the occupants of a UFO.

Mrs Jean Hingley of Bluestone Walk of Blackheath says that she met not only met creatures from outer space, but actually invited them into her home.

A police investigation has so far drawn a blank, but Chief Superintendent Mellor of Sandwell Police said that Jean seems "a very sane lady" — and Jean is convinced about what she saw.

She said: "It may sound strange but I'd swear on the Holy Bible that it is the truth.

Jean's experience occurred at 7 o'clock in the morning after her husband Cyril had left for work.

"I went to the door to let the dog out when there was a sudden blinding light.

"I was stunned and I tried to speak but my mouth just opened and no words came out.

"I told myself I must pull myself together, that it was not real. But then I looked at the dog and he seemed paralysed. His hair was standing on end and seemed to spread in all directions."

If Jean then described a strange humming sound and the arrival of three alien creatures.

Three green men came towards me and into the kitchen. They had beautiful rainbow coloured wings and seemed to fly, not walk.

Jean described her visitors as having pointed heads, hands and feet and being about three feet high.

She said that they were silvery-green clothing which glowed, and their faces were pale and composite.

They were very interested in touching things, and examined the lounge and the Christmas tree.

"But they became terrified when I lit a cigarette, and they ran back in their space-craft, which Jean described as a scorpion-shaped object covered in a plastic skin and glowing brightly.

She watched as the craft rose into the early morning sky and disappeared towards Dudley.

Jean said it was definitely not ballustinating and I can only believe what I saw with my own eyes."

They had pasty white faces, and wore green suits.

They were not green men.

Mrs Jean Hingley and her dog . . . "I can only believe what I saw with my own eyes."

Mario Luisi - Cumbria. England

On Tuesday, the 25th November 1980, the Lancashire Evening Post carried a story of Mario Luisi a paper mill worker, who had encountered humanoids at Burnside, Cumbria on the 21st November at 8.00p.m. My daughter-in-law Celia sent me the article, asking if I would like to go and interview him.

A while after Celia and I did get to motoring up to Cumbria and spent a day with Mario. He proved to be quite an amiable young man, with a soft voice. Under certain circumstances I felt, he could be pretty tough, having been an Army PT instructor. Fortuitously, Mario's teenage daughter from Preston was visiting the same day, we were able to offer a lift back to gain more of an insight of her father, she informed us he was afraid of nothing, inclined to fist first and think afterwards! But whatever it was he experienced, it had scared the daylights out of him, she personally did not believe in UFOs and all that.

Burnside is a pretty little Lake District village; it is cleft in half by a deep river gorge and a weir, a small factory, the paper mill on one bank, with a Council estate behind it. The river rights and a lot of land are owned by some Lord or another, as is the case in England. His bailiffs see to it that men do not poach salmon from the river. There is an ancient Celtic mound by the other bank, and a cattle field beyond this. Mario had a new torch and was in this field, looking for his fishing tackle, which he had dropped by the mound earlier, when he noticed what he thought, was a cattle pen, then a cow in the centre of the very mushy field. Then he heard a rustling by a large oak tree there, and two people in wetsuits appeared in front of, what he now saw was a small craft about 16ft x 8 ft deep coloured, with a glass like window to the front. They were beautiful looking people about his height. They had fair hair in a helmet style, which puzzled him, for although there was a strong wind their hair did not move at all. Their skins were very pale. He now from feeling startled began to feel terrified, 'she' had a slim torch in her hand, and she pointed it at his torch and disintegrated it. Then promptly told him, they wouldn't harm him.

These Beings had appeared as startled at seeing him as he was them, they were only with him a few minutes, during which she did all the talking. She said they came from the sky, and he was not to tell anyone about their insignia. She wore a cloak. When I asked-how did you know the being was a 'she', he said 'I looked at her breasts of course! She was well covered, quite plump' - a typical Mario reaction. He was what one would term "Quite a lad!" though in that moment he was in a blue funk, he wanted to run, but was glued to the spot. 'Then they got in the ship, it had folding stairs and shot straight into the sky, leaving a red glow on a cloud'.

Mario then virtually flew off that field; his wife was out, so he ran over to his Mother's. She had a neighbour there who promptly informed the Police, who sent a Constable out to see Mario, the local press were then told of this. Mario himself had not wanted to inform any media or authority. The experience so unnerved him, he felt unable to move out of his house for weeks.

On Wednesday, the 12th August 1981 between 10.30p.m - 10.45p.m. Mario, his wife and another couple, friends of theirs were returning from an outing over Shap Fells, when the car light went out, it stopped and they thought it was the alternator giving trouble. Then they noticed two men standing in the centre of the road, coming towards them, they had on light coloured zip-suits and wore helmets with visors over the eyes. It was misty, drizzling with rain and the women started to yell. Quite calmly Mario told them to 'keep the windows and doors shut, they want me, not you'. He walked out and accompanied the two Beings towards the mountainside. He then appears to have passed out, for the next thing he was in a glass box, in a room with roof and walls all the same light colour, which seemed to glow from within, the corners were rounded. When asked if he was confined, he said no it was roomy, there was about four feet either side of him, and he noticed now another such box containing someone, whose leg was only visible to him. He could move his arms, but his head was fixed. To the other side he could see a shelf of glass above him, and on this were boxes, parts of which were black, he could see into the fronts. One contained a rabbit, and another a small mammal of some sort, the third to his amazement contained a single dandelion standing up!

Having listened many times over, to these absurd inconsistencies in the stories abductees tell, this incongruous bit of information to my mind seemed to give a whole ring of authenticity to Mario's story, abduction lore is littered with them.

At this, Mario said he became aware that there were 6 people flitting in and out of the room, they came and went through a sliding door. Three of the men were between 5ft 6ins and 5ft 10 ins, the two women were 5ft 4 ins to 5ft 6 ins. approx. All of these had on one-piece suits which were light coloured, and helmets with holes in them. They were ordinary looking people, no different to us. A sixth man of about 5ft 6 ins and looked older, about 50 years, came and spoke to him. He told him not to be afraid, they had come a long way to learn, and he had been chosen to be a Counsellor. The planet they came from was called Sorben, about the same size as our Earth. He spoke good English and his mouth moved when talking. Strangely this time Mario said he felt quite calm. When asked if they were the same people he met the year before in the November of 1980, he said they looked much the same, but he did not know.

There was some sort of TV (or scan) screen above him, on which his insides showed up. Mario it seemed had no recollection of entering or leaving the craft, if indeed there was a craft, he never saw one. His next recollection is of walking towards his car in drizzle and mist. He looked back and all he could see was trees and mist. If he had been on his own, he said, he would have felt he was dreaming, but his wife and the other couple had seen him leave with the two men. When he got in the car the other lady was in hysterics and he smacked her to calm her down, they were saying it was 11.50p.m. 'What have you been doing'?

When the North Lancashire and South Cumbria UFO Investigations Group contacted him Mario told them he had asked this couple to tell them about the incident, but they had said they would deny it. His wife also denied it.

On the occasion of our visit, Mario's wife who flitted in and out of the Living Room, supplying us with cups of tea, was non-committal. She neither confirmed nor denied any of the snatches of conversation she obviously heard. Most of the time she shut her children and herself in the kitchen, whilst we were there or out examining the field and river. One could see that the household was feeling the pinch of unemployment, money was very tight. There was one small bookcase in the Living Room, from which Mario brought out a UFO book, which he said he had got from Kendal Library.

Mario then told us we could contact Father Taylor or Osmond at Black Hall Road, Catholic Church Kendal, as he had gone to them for advice, they had believed him. These priests had said they did not know anything about the subject, but were willing to read any book I recommended, he had told them of my impending visit.

The local UFO Group had lent Mario considerable support, and I did not wish to intrude upon their investigations, though as this case seemed to progress, they began to feel out of their depth and wrote also phoned, asking for my advice. I in turn contacted Timothy Good; this is standard procedure in our UFO circles. Mario now complained that the BEINGS were taking him over, appearing in his bedroom and imparting all sorts of messages, they enjoined him to give to 'his leaders'. Mario said his wife would be in a deep sleep beside him, she however, now denied this could be happening. Again one does hear of this sort of happening from all over the world.

About the only leader I could think of was the Earl of Clancarty. I asked Timothy to approach him, and I would contact him also. Initially the Earl agreed and said he would invite his House of Lords Study Group to his house privately to meet this man. No doubt after consultations with his colleagues he withdrew this, rather naively 'Why did THEY not contact the Leaders of this World, instead of a poor, uneducated, unemployed man, tell him to tell them to come to London!"

In the meantime Timothy Good and I had gone to the trouble of arranging to finance Mario's train fare down to London. The situation had become theatrical and farcical, for Mario it seemed in sheer desperation that some contactees develop for attention, had donned a silver foil suit, and got his relative to take two photos with a bit of trick photography, purporting them to be the aliens.

At this Tim Good was determined to go and investigate himself It was a very severe winter, the weather was appalling with thick snow and ice as Tim heroically ventured North to Kendal. After an almost impossible journey he installed himself in a Hotel in Kendal, where Mario's sister visited him and spilt the beans. At this Tim returned home disillusioned and. rejected Mario altogether. This trick of Mario's certainly set me back as well, I felt embarrassed that it had spoilt my credibility with the Earl of Clancarty and his Group, although the English Class system being what it is, I was unlikely to ever meet any of them. I did feel my reputation threatened, then abject letters of remorse and apology followed from Mario, he said he knew he should never have done it, but being so badly off financially, he had given away to temptation, and also he had stupidly thought he could convince them the more.

I had to give this a lot of thought. Timothy was quite adamant that having been asked to investigate, he was entitled to form a moral judgement. I on the other hand think it matters not whether we consider a witness good or bad, as long as we feel the report is genuine, our judgements of character cannot invalidate this. With Timothy I decided it was best for us to drop the case, but I knew that would not be the end of it for me.

When I settled down in Wales I periodically decided to keep in touch with Mario to see what, if anything would develop. Occasionally Mario would write to say the information they were giving him was unbelievable - but he was hard up and if anyone wanted this information they would have to pay for it.

I would ignore these letters. Eventually my persistence paid off at the cost of disillusionment with human nature. Mario got a job and his circumstances improved. Finally he admitted the subsequent events were invented but he persists to this day that the initial encounter on the 21st November 1980 at Burnside took place. I am inclined to believe it did. This affected Mario so profoundly that he embroidered on what initially happened in order to strengthen his story; or perhaps in all honesty it was the desperate desire to make money. Unemployment demoralises people. Mario admits this caused embarrassment and inconvenience to Timothy Good and myself and he made no excuses for himself. He did at least have the courage to say I may write this in my book. The reader may judge for himself.

NOTE: Investigators - Margaret Fry and Timothy Good

The North Lancashire UFO Investigation Group - The 'Luisi' Case Preliminary report on torch

From the positions of the damaged areas of the torch, it could be assumed with reasonable certainty that the whole torch was intact when the damage occurred. That is, the distortion on the surrounding area of the plastic component that held the glass is consistent with what would be expected were the central portion subjected to a certain degree of heat.

The main component of interest is the reflector, having sustained the most visible effects. This reflector would seem to be basically composed of a thermoplastic, electroplated with chrome - or, more likely, sprayed with a thin coating of chrome to a density of not more than 7 microns (0,0015").

The reflector is most likely a polyacetal (formaldehyde polymer) plastic, which has a good heat resistance and excellent dimensional stability. Alternatively, a polypropylene plastic has an even better heat resistance - (service temperatures are in excess of 100°C, /Melting point - about 145°C.). Temperatures above 65°C after moulding distort most plastics.

In heavy plastic plating the object is immersed in a solution of copper in sulphuric acid for between 2 - 5 minutes at a current density around 5A/sq.ft. to cover contact areas with
enough copper to withstand higher densities in the main plating solution.

It would seem most likely that the damage was effected by some form of electrical discharge or something of like nature.

For simple physical heat, temperatures in excess of 65°C would be necessary. This would also tend to blacken the plastic and leave sooty deposits - none of which is in evidence in this particular case.

To achieve such an effect by means of a blow-torch would require it to be set at a very high temperature for a very short period or time - but this would also tend to distort the surrounding plastic of the casing, making it very difficult to achieve an effect similar to that of the Luisi torch. However, a form of relatively 'cold' heat - such as with an oxy-acetylene torch would produce more favourable results. This would, though, imply an ingenious and elaborate hoax, which, in the Luisi case, appears most unlikely.

In conclusion, it would appear that the source (electrical, or other) of the damage could be compared to a 'tube' of heat (see fig.), in which the highest temperature or point of power is concentrated in a localised area, and the perimeter of that 'tube' would have a much lower temperature or lesser charge, thus accounting for the minimal damage occasioned to the surrounding area of the casing.

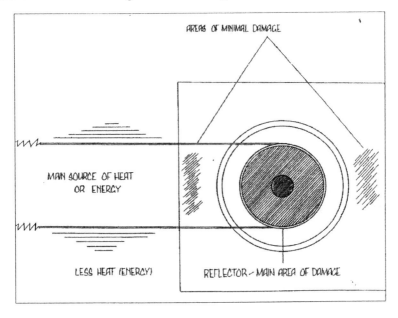

Diagram showing the damage to Mario Luisi's torch

Article in the Lancashire Evening Post describing Mario Luisi's encounter with Humanoids

Mrs. Sage. Kent. England

The area where these people lived was a small hamlet outside the main town of Chatham, in the Medway countryside. I gathered buses were few and far between, so that the women on this small Estate lead the isolated lives of a small village, although their men folk worked in the main Chatham catchment.

On this particular afternoon the 4th August 1980, the winds were strong in the morning and it rained. By the afternoon these had died down. It was still alternately sunny then clouding over. At 4.40p.m. by the kitchen clock, Marie Louise Mrs Sage's daughter was watching a children's programme on TV called Blue Peter. Her son, 20 years old, was in the Living Room, and she was preparing the evening meal, for her husband always arrived home at 5.40p.m. invariably very hungry and wanting his evening meal. At this she realised she had run out of peas, and asked the son to run up to the small row of shops on a hill above the Estate, but he refused. Rather than waste time arguing with him, she hastily put on her check coat, took 20p from her purse and hurried out of the house. As she climbed the 7 ft wide concrete steps of the Alley behind the back gardens, she was half way up when she was startled to see there was a ring of smoke around her neighbour's roof Out of this came a craft, somewhat the shape of a helicopter, but with no propellers, there were two men in it. She had to pass a bricks and mortar shed at the bottom of her neighbour's garden to get an unobstructed view between the two houses.

Now she could see the craft as it came down to the level of the rear bushes. It had a glassed-in front, which these men slid open. There was also a small shutter at the side of the craft, which opened and made a Click-click sound. They were virtually feet from her. She said "Oh you frightened me" and they laughed, "What did she say?" the other answered "Oh - we frightened her, let's get on with the Job we were going to do", then the craft turned towards the gap between the houses.

The craft was similar in shape to those bulky Army helicopters, and about their size, it was approximately 4ft. to 5 ft. wide. It was camouflaged in motley greens and browns, but it made no sound at all. The glassed front where the men sat had metal levers. One of them had dark hair, the other fair, both had short men's haircuts and a dark tan, "They were not coloured men, just deeply tanned," she said. They had on one-piece dark grey suits, which seemed to have no zips or pockets. The whole of the front of the craft was glassed. When thinking over this many months later, Mrs. Sage felt she had stood there 14 minutes 10 seconds, which she calculated very carefully by retracing her steps.

At this Mrs. Sage hurried on to the shops above to buy her peas. When she came out she met a friend, and stood to talk for about five minutes, during which this Lady asked her if she knew her niece had got married. Then Mrs. Sage hurried down the steps, she had hesitated at the top, but did not want to get late to go the long way round by another road. As she went down the fair man was standing by the bushes lining the bottom of her neighbour's garden, he was bending down, but straightened up as she drew level and smiled. She thought 'Don't think I'm going to think you are Army, because I don't'.

On returning indoors all this wiped out of Mrs. Sage's mind. Her son was upstairs, and her young daughter informed her the television had stopped going whilst she was away, but had now come back on. She had left the potatoes cooking on a low gas, so she went to check these and glanced at the clock. Presumably she felt on schedule, for on coming home her husband remarked he was five minutes early, the kitchen clock must be slow, so he adjusted it. So that we did not know if she had lost any time at all, if she did, the most it would have been would have been 20 minutes. Because of the buses from Chatham, the husband always arrived home at 5.40p.m. from work.

When they were all seated at the table for supper, she remembered the conversation with her friend, and told her husband her niece had got married without telling them.

Six weeks later her neighbour and her daughter told her about two policemen in Scotland who had seen what looked like an airship. This rang a bell with her, and she felt puzzled that she had seen something strange as well, but where? Then two days later the memory of the smoke above the neighbour's house, and the strange helicopter came back to her

This brought on severe trauma of bouts of terrible headaches and vomiting for six weeks after, during which period she felt weak and dazed.

This made her recall that on seeing the blond man at the bottom of her neighbour's garden, there had been a mist over the bushes and a strong, sweet smell which had made her very sick. The smell was not of flowers, but really strong. For weeks after she now recalled she had felt lifeless with headaches. She had not associated these with what she had seen, as at the time she had no memory of it. During this period she also felt unusually thirsty, this bout had also lasted 6 weeks. Mrs Sage had never suffered from headaches before and she did not have dreams or nightmares. In fact during that period of feeling ill, she slept very badly due to her nausea, and she frequently got up and went downstairs in the night, when her husband would bring her cups of tea.

At some stage during the following months my friend Patricia Grant a UFO investigator had heard of her and contacted the family. All the memories of that day only came back gradually over a period of months well into the following year for Mrs. Sage. As she recalled things she would get very upset and they seemed to pose a threat to her, so that one wonders whether more occurred that lies deep in her subconscious which has never surfaced?

Mrs. Sage did not think that any of her other neighbours had seen the craft, but all the women living near her had noticed all the changes that occurred in the alley and their gardens, and were talking about them. The concrete steps of the Alley had been 7 ft, wide enough to take a woman with a baby's pram, plus a friend walking alongside, now it had narrowed to allow for one-person passage. The alley itself seemed to have lengthened. The 5th to 6th step up had been wider than the others; it was now the same width as all the steps. The neighbour, who had a back fence with a gate, now had neither, only a row of overgrown cotton wool bushes. The bricks and mortar shed at the base of garden of the neighbour the other side had just shifted from the bottom to the centre of the garden! The large old tree with thick branches just outside Mr. K's back door had simply vanished overnight, with no ground disturbance to show it had ever been there.

The neighbours had always noticed that this family had taken little interest in their back yard. It was now neatly lawned, not with new or turfed grass, but grass that looked as though it had been established years. All the hedging in that area of the Estate had burnt down in July 1979. Now a neatly growing privet was growing, and a fully-grown mature tree had appeared in the lawn.

Now all this was pretty difficult to digest. Mrs Sage and four women neighbours who were all discussing these changes were bewildered and thinking they were going 'bonkers'. She asked a male neighbour Mr B... to go and examine all areas, and give his opinion. He did, and was so bewildered, he actually took it upon himself to write independently to Pat the UFO investigator. At another time almost all the neighbours had noticed a large sprawling building which seemed to just appear on the Downs opposite the Estate, where there had been bare slopes of grass. Apart from the peculiarities of the case, it is quite unique in so far as various neighbours and the boy's employer went out of their way to not only see, but also write to verify what the bewildered Sage family was telling the Investigator.

During the course of the investigation, which lasted well into 1981, various paranormal happenings were occurring in the Sage household, such as voices holding clear conversations in the house, with what they described as slurry robot like voices, but no one was seen. During this time the housedogs would bark incessantly.

Gradually over the months as this Lady consciously remembered snatches from this incident, she recalled that when she had seen the fair man by the bushes on her return journey, she had also seen the craft hovering inches over her neighbour's garden. The dark haired man was in it, and standing in front was one blond and one dark haired man, both 4ft 5ins in height they both had fair skins, as opposed to the tanned pilots. She saw the glassed partition slide open and heard one say 'this is my brother', the man in the craft took his hand. At this Mrs. Sage now felt strongly these two men were her neighbour Mr. K. and his brother, although both wore glasses and these men did not. She felt so afraid she walked away quickly.

In correspondence to the Investigator, she frequently mentions that she saw the craft back down into the bushes. This is most baffling, when she felt sure it was 4ft. to 5ft wide, and she felt as long as an average helicopter. She mentions too, that since the bushes had overgrown, her neighbour and the daughter now had to walk down past the alley and turn up the road below to go to their front door, whereas they previously had gone in from the back gate, which now appeared to have disappeared altogether. When she mentioned this, she was told there never had been a back gate. She admits that she hardly knew Mr. K. by appearance, she had been told he had a twin brother, who did not resemble him at all, but she had never met him. She had noted Mr. K's smallness of stature, and again had been told the brother was the same height.

On the 13th December 1980 she her family and some of the neighbours heard a low humming sound, they went outside but could see nothing. This made Mrs Sage recall the small incident of her husband returning 5 minutes early on the 4th August 1980, and adjusting the slow kitchen clock.

As to the reactions of Mrs. Sage's immediate family there are many letters on file of one son's total faith in what his Mother had experienced. He had himself previously seen a UFO when at work and been derided by his work-mates. I do not know how the 2nd son reacted; the daughter was possibly too young and accepted matters. Her husband at first listened to Mrs. Sage when she would recall various parts of the Incident, but when she said the craft was painted in camouflage mottled colours of greens and browns, that passed his credulity level. He exploded in annoyance 'No craft could enter through the Earth's atmosphere without the paint burning off'. Thereafter, she decided not to tell him anything further.

Pat the investigator decided that in the interests of trying to understand this baffling phenomenon, she should befriend and keep in touch with this very ordinary working class lady. Their friendship has continued now for the past 16 years. Eventually most of the changes that occurred in that small Estate returned to normal, with the exception of the alley, which is still narrower. Mrs. Sage who was in the midst of all these extraordinary happenings, has continued to lead an ordinary life, beset with the usual joys and sorrows. She has lost her husband and moved to a smaller house; her life continues on an even keel, she has never experienced anything further

I would point out to my readers, that on the 17th January 1978 I too had a ring of clover in my back garden turn to ordinary grass overnight. Not new, not patched-in grass, just grass that looked as though it had always been there. Tim Good would verify this. So what do I make of the saga of Mrs Sage?

This is in no way derogatory, neither the Sages nor their neighbours on this little Council Estate were well-educated people; they were working class factory or manual workers. If they had previously heard of UFOs, it was through the occasional newspaper report. So why would they have hallucinated all these extraordinary happenings? None of Mrs Sage's neighbours had doubted her encounter, in view of the later inexplicable changes. Over the years others have struggled to explain this distortion of dimensions, time and Space due to the UFO phenomena, I have myself, but nowhere was this so dramatically indicated by so many witnesses, as in this Chatham case.

It is something that seems to drive the more scientifically minded UFO buffs, and people who do not know a thing about the phenomenon alike, to a vindictive frenzy, and it is not something the poor unfortunate victim of it can vigorously defend, because you are reeling yourself with disbelief that such a thing can happen in our three dimensional world. I put this on a par with seeing ghosts, if you have seen one you believe, if you haven't you can't.

Yet, maybe as our world technologically advances, this will be perfectly scientifically explainable in fifty to a hundred years' time.

Mrs Sage's sketch of the craft

NOTE: *Investigators - Patricia Grant and Timothy Good*

Jayne (pseudonym) - South Wales

The interview was one of the most difficult I have ever undertaken, firstly because we had to travel the best part of seven hours getting down to the tip of South Wales from the North. The whole of Wales is mountainous and wild though beautiful, you either go along steep winding tracks or over into Shropshire, Herefordshire and then back into South Wales, either way it's a long tiring journey. Added to this the witness hadn't really wanted to see me, she had heard Jenny Randles on BBC Radio Wales on the 22nd April 1991 and wanted to speak to her.

I had to explain that each of us investigated cases in our own area, and I happened to be the Investigator coordinator for Contact International UK for Wales, and at that time also for BUFORA, Miss Randles who was the then Head of Investigators for BUFORA could not be everywhere. Well, she reluctantly agreed to see me instead, but I was to take no notes or the names of the places she wanted me to see. At this point Jayne made it clear we would have a meal firstly, before disclosing anything. She was an attractive lady, I guessed about 50, and she had married children and some grandchildren. Later from the dates she gave I realised she was possibly 60. She asked me about my investigative experience and I told her about some of my Kent cases and also Welsh ones, she was summing me up, and would have certainly asked me to go, had she decided I was not trustworthy or experienced enough for her! She struck me as being a quite determined and practical lady. She had been through some personal stress at deciding to confide in Jenny Randles, let alone a substitute for her.

My husband is now disabled and does not get out of the car when taking me to UFO investigations, he is a very patient person and would rather sit listening to his radio, than make the effort of getting out and into a wheelchair, which he loathes. So I might say I too was summing up this stranger, and marks went to her when she said 'we must go and check your poor patient husband first, and get him something to eat and drink, also your dog! We did this and she asked Ron if he would mind motoring her to various places she wanted to show me, she would pay the petrol. We agreed, but declined the petrol money and after the meal set off

We motored some distance from this seaside resort out into the country, where we were taken to a very pretty area of low hills and farms, we then drove on her direction through a narrow country lane to a farm, with some houses opposite it. Jayne said these had not been there when she was young, only one belonging to the family of her small friend, up the road from them. Opposite a large old whitewashed farmhouse we stopped. Two country lane roads forked out in front of this, and as in her childhood there was open farming land behind. She had not been there since. We got out and walked up the lane, as she looked for the house of her friend. The house still stood, it was smallish and red brick, but the garden and entrance were completely changed. She wanted to find some Steps leading to a gate that opened to an acre of vegetable plot, but there was nothing left of this. The large several acres of farmland and row of trees along the end of the original vegetable plot were still there. On seeing this, tears rolled down her eyes, she said 'can we turn back'. So we walked back to the tied cottage her parents had rented and which was much smaller when they had lived in it (in 1934 approx. I was not given the exact year).

Now these are the disjointed but vivid memories of a 2½-3 year-old child. Her little friend was very dark and had an unusual face, so did her family. She was 6½ years old, but the only other girl there, her brothers were younger but rough to play with. Most afternoons Jayne played with the 6½ year old, name not given. She would have to return home for tea about 4.30p.m.

On this particular afternoon in the summer of approximately 1934 Jayne trotted the few yards up the road, it was hot as she walked up a small hill incline and went towards the back of the semi-detached house. She found the kitchen door open, but no one there. This half her friend, 2 small brothers, mother and father lived, a concrete path was right across the backs of the two semi-detached as the grandparents lived the other side, where she now went to their back kitchen door. Their door was also open and no one there. She then went back to the side of the house, where there were 3 steps to the large vegetable plot. She thought it was about an acre and the area she pointed out to me seemed so, with a line of large oak or sycamore trees down one side dividing it from open fields. She was hot and sat for a while on the top step, then cautiously she opened the gate and went in. The Father had forbidden the children to play there. Now she saw a row of beans, which seemed to have eyes peering at her (Beans are ripe in July/August). She timidly went past them, then seeing a group of people some distance away, she hurried towards them, when she caught up there were 'soldiers', in green/grey siren suits. She did not think this unusual, as all the farm workers wore siren suits, and later in the war years everyone wore them. However these soldiers had ray guns (please note again, this is a childhood memory and she expressed herself as she thought then). They were pushing along the hapless family, who were very reluctantly and slowly complying. She rushed at one of the men's legs, and said, "Leave my friend alone". He shoved her forward with the rest.

She now noticed a "big silver caravan behind the trees in the field". They were sent up some steps into it, and the door shut. Again she rushed at 'a soldier's' trousers. "Don't hurt my friend, leave her be". The soldiers had what seemed like rounded tin helmets on. They also had belts with some gadget in the centre, and all carried this ray gun. She now saw they were in a large room, with many people standing like statues, apart from the soldiers. As she persisted in tugging the soldier's leg and begging for her friend and herself, she was lifted and dumped with the family. Now she heard the Father say, "You can see she is obviously not mine, she belongs to a family down the road, let her go". Eventually after a haggle, which went over her head, she was lifted, shoved through the door and it slid shut. She found herself running past the vegetables, past the beans that seemed to have eyes and opened the gate, and then sat down on the top step again.

There she sat for a "very long time" it had been 3.45p.m. when she had gone to the house, but now it was getting dark as she stiffly got up and looked towards the trees, but the silver caravan had gone. She was very upset about her friend, thinking she had no one left to play with. Then she realised it was long past home going time, so she hurried up the lane. Her father was at the gate, he picked her up and hugged her, then he started shaking her "Where have you been, its long past 6 o'clock, long past teatime, Mammy and I, and all the farm workers have been looking all over for you". "I was with my friend, but she was not there, soldiers took them all away'. Mother said "You sat on her garden step all this time? We are going right now to Mrs. X to tell her how inconsiderate she is. Why didn't she send you home for tea? She must have known we were worried". "Come with me, I'm going over to see her". "But Mam, she was taken away by soldiers". "What soldiers, there are no soldiers here, come on". So she took her hand and walked up the hill to the two semi-detached houses, but on inspection she saw they were both empty.

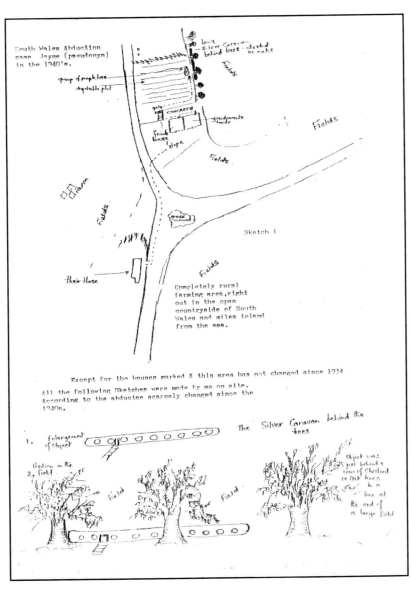

Sketches made by me on site of Jayne's (pseudonym) abduction

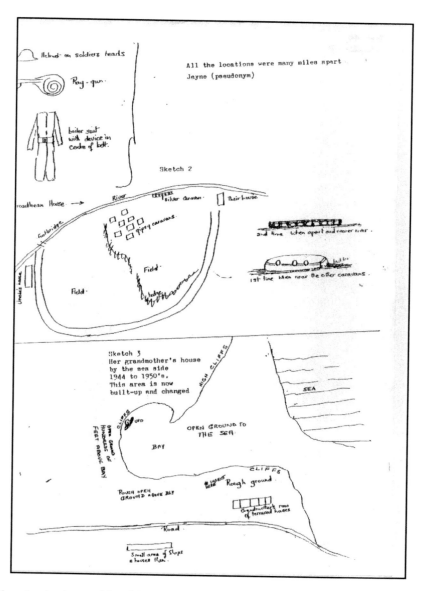

More sketches by me of the abduction site and Jayne's recollection of the soldiers' uniform'

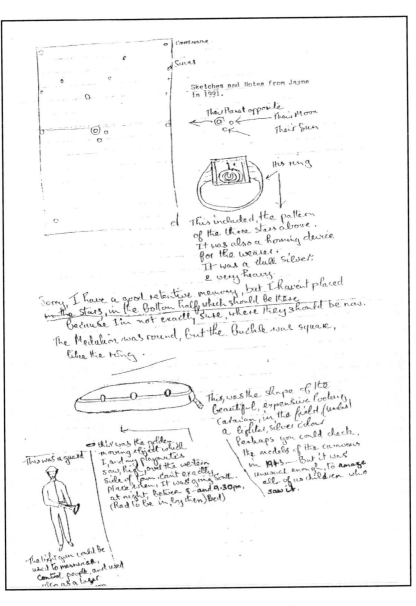

Jayne's sketches and notes (1991)

I now asked if her mother recalled this "Yes", she said, "She is still alive and when I was a child she did on a few occasions wonder where that whole family had disappeared to. But you must remember these are my memories of a 2½-3 year old child, coming here has revived some of it, but it is still only spasmodic, I don't remember it all in sequence, so please accept that I will jump about a bit, as I remember things. Years later as this re-occurred in my childhood, I decided I was having vivid dreams, and that all this was a dream".

The following year or after a few years from what she can recall, they shifted because her father took another job, so lost the tied cottage. They went to live in a house owned by her Uncle. Broadbean House ... This was in a very rural setting, even more so than Swanbridge Lane, there was a small semi-circular lane leading to her Uncle's farmhouse, with two large fields between them. The houses were not visible to each other; the fields and houses were flanked on one side by a river.

Each summer her Uncle permitted the gypsies to park in the field nearer their house, they helped out on the farm. She and her cousins sometimes talked to the gipsy children. Her Uncle liked and was liked by the gypsies. On this occasion, she thought it must have been in the early days of the War, but did not remember exactly when, she was walking down the lane to her Uncle's house, when she looked across at the group of gipsy caravans, when she noticed one much larger, and richer looking "caravan" in silver, parked apart from them by the river. She wondered who was rich enough to own such a van, as the day before something had happened which she vividly recalls in detail to this day.

Her Mother always sent her to school with jam sandwiches for Lunch, which she absolutely hated. When after school she cut across a footbridge over the river, she walked into the field where the gipsy children were, as she was allowed to talk to them, she was talking to a little boy. She had been unwrapping the hated sandwiches to throw in the river, when she noticed the expression on his face. The sandwiches were all squashed and horrible, and seeing her house in the distance she was hesitating between gulping them down or pitching them away, when she looked at his big eyes and really noticed how ragged and thin he was. He said, "if you don' t want them, can I have them?" and he just gulped them down. "Doesn't your Mam feed you?" "Doesn't your Mam have any food coupons to feed you?" "We are gypsies, we are not allowed to have coupons". This left a very deep and lasting impression on her principles in life. I said, "That would have been during the War?" Yes I think it was May 1943, when I try to go back in my mind about it. At the moment my mind is going back and forth, trying to remember for you. I think I was taken into one of these silver caravans when I was also about 6, but I want to tell you now about when I was 10 or 11 years old I think. I want to tell you about this now ... because this evening when I was walking down to my Uncle's house to play with my cousins, it was dusk. And I saw this caravan. It was a few days, no 2 weeks later, as I think it was now June 1943, because by this time the gipsy caravans had left, and they always left by June. There was this long, long silver caravan, with a row of a lot of windows sitting in the field where the gipsy vans had been. I think the windows were round, but I'm not sure of that. Some weeks before in May, I had seen something that looked like a silver disc or a helmet sitting near the gipsy vans, but nearer the river. I thought then one of the gypsies must have been much richer than the rest, because I thought of the starving little boy who ate my sandwiches. But this time it was bigger, still and long, not the same shape, so I thought they had to be very rich. So naturally I felt so curious, I walked down the field in the gathering dark, I did not feel afraid. The lights were the only bright ones there. There were no streetlights between my Uncle's house and ours in the lane between, and no other lights anywhere. Our house and my Uncle's house had gas lighting, which wasn't half as bright.

As I was walking down the field towards the caravan, a man and a woman came up on either side of me. They wore the same green/grey boiler suits, one had the same ray gun in his hand. I felt forced to walk with them. They took me up to a door, and I was shut in with them. I could not move, I was now very afraid; because when walking towards the caravan with them I had seen 80-90 people all from Broadbean Street, standing like statues outside the caravan, guarded by the boiler-suited men with ray guns pointed at them.

This was the one occasion I insisted upon interrupting. This conversation was taking place in a very rocky but extra pretty little cove, which she had asked Ron to drive to, near by to this area of her first abduction. Again after ensuring Ron had a drink etc. in the car, we had carefully picked our way down to the sea with my dog. The sole interruptions had been to make sure my dog did not stray too far. It was sunny but quite windy, so I now asked if we could move to sitting in a more sheltered spot, which we did behind some large rocks. I asked if she was sure there had been 80-90 people there? "Oh yes," she said, "I recognised many of them, the butcher, the baker, milkman, shop people, people down that street, I used to go to school in the area. And afterwards I longed to ask them if they remembered."

This lady was so reticent about herself, her family and background that I felt it would not have taken much for her to have stopped talking altogether. We had motored a very long way, at some expense to interview her, so I put up with the discomfort of sitting in the wind facing the Bristol Channel, as she talked. Often tears streamed down her eyes, as her memories became too painful. Although we were taken to most of the localities where she had these experiences, we stopped where she requested and hardly had the chance of finding out where we were. I was cramped up on the back seat with my dog and luggage which was not conducive to observing much, and Ron has a hopelessly poor sense of direction, I always navigate him. So as far as we observed, her localities are still secret even to us! So wild horses could not even drag them from me! Every so often she was adamant that she did not want ridicule for herself, her family, or her family being told secondhand and disbelieving her, she'd rather they never knew, not even her husband.

Every so often she would go up avenues of thought that she would shut up abruptly and say she was not going to tell me, that I simply would not believe her, or I would think she was mad, which she certainly was not. No, I did not think her mad, suddenly she would use a turn of phrase which would startle me, and I would think of Rae Fountain, Jean Hingley, Irene Williams, the boys in Barnehurst in 1978, and I would know she has the common factor in her which they all have, and which Ron and I instinctively know now, though we could not express it, or pin point it. With them, she has been to hell and back and who are we to gainsay it?

When I asked what happened to the 80-90 people, she said she did not know, because this was the first time she saw somebody she called in her mind The Khan, he wore an ornate ring, was tall and far more like a good-looking person. The others, the boiler-suited, helmeted men were always about 4ft. with grey/white skins, very small, but diamond looking eyes (please note she had never read about Jean Hingley. I gathered she had read some of Erich Von Daniken which she thought defective, 1 or 2 others and Timothy Good's books). "These men's eyes were somewhat slanted, but not like Chinese, they had a thin line for mouths. But I never thought of them as aliens then, as this was the war and everyone wore boiler suits, the farm workers -everyone. I was only 10 or 11 years old". When she was taken into the caravan, the Khan came up to her, he said "when you were small with your friend, she and her family were ours. We come from Cons Major. We do not have leaders". He told her many things. If she tried to remember it all, it would take several days telling, he told her they had programmed her from the first time. At this stage, she really wept and then she said she was sorry she could not go on, she said ... and "they did a lot of things to me".

We then got up and went up to a patio type of area, where there was a Pub and food and drinks kiosk. We stopped for drinks and for her to smoke, then we walked towards the parking area where Ron was, and whilst walking she said 'you see all those years ago, they kept telling me they would not harm me. I had to convince myself I was having re-occurring bad dreams in order to live with it ... but then after I got a job, I had my first boyfriend at 21 years of age, and we were abducted together, so I had to acknowledge to myself that all these things in my childhood really happened. You see now since NASA and all these American probes have gone up, as I've heard what they have discovered, I know they are not telling half the truth, the Khan told me there was an anti-matter world near them. You can imagine how I felt when Voyager II went past the satellites of Pluto. He also said there was an anti-matter world alongside us, and to interfere with this, would destroy our whole universe.

Here she tried to explain to me about this anti-gravity and what could happen, but as I was permitted to make no notes and I scarcely understood what she was talking about, so I just don't remember half of what was said. She appeared to understand some of what she recalled being told. When we went to the Pub to get tea, she made some comments that made me realise she is normally quite an assertive lady with her family, bar her husband. Jayne appears to fall into the traditional Welsh pattern of husband making all the decisions so he did not permit her to work, she had only concentrated on bringing up her large family. She appeared to have no outside interests beyond her family and Chapel. This is the normal here, so that is why I know she has only read Tim Good's book and Von Daniken etc. I don't think she would go out of the way to do anything out of the ordinary. She was not the type of person who had friends and invited them over to her house. She liked dogs, fussed over and considered the needs of mine, and that was all she talked about in public places, restaurants and before my husband. When driving Ron to all these localities, she back-seat drove most forcefully, but laughed at herself, saying the family all told her she was shocking in a car, when we left her Ron had a good laugh and said "come back Margaret, all is forgiven. My word, I couldn't put up with that for long!"

So I must say here, this Investigation, this extraordinary investigation could not have taken place without the wholehearted cooperation of my ever-patient husband. He had sat in the car good-natured and patiently waiting for hours listening to his radio and taking us wherever this Lady wanted.

When we had got to the next location in a different town, it was a built up area with high cliffs in a semi-circular bay. She had by now recovered from her emotion in the cove. She did in fact describe The Khan in detail, small sketch enclosed. The ring he had bore a design of the position of their planet to their sun, he wore a tunic, with a white oblong across the chest which had the same design an the ring, the circles he had on these formed a rough letter 5, with semi-circles in the base. He explained the significance of this to her. Here she said no one would believe half of what he had told her the repeated times she met him. Or had he invented only what they had wanted to inform her of, she had often wondered, once she had reached adulthood. Other people had always shared these experiences with her, her boyfriend, her husband, her brother, but she had not the courage to say, "you were there, don't you remember, have you not the courage to talk of it either?"

113

During this part of the conversation I very much wanted to ask her why she thought a 12 year old child like her had been selected for all this knowledge, when 80-90 of her fellow adults seemed to have been by-passed. A quite baffling thought, but this lady brooked few interruptions once she got talking about these abductions. When she was with Ron she was far more hesitant, saying we had been very kind and patient and she had to honestly say given the reverse of positions she would not have been, she would then listen to what we were both saying, but once alone with me, she simply wanted to get as much as possible out of her system, and didn't want to be questioned or interrupted, which was thoroughly exhausting both for me and herself

After the Khan incident, which happened when she was 10/11 years old, many nights she would see from her bedroom window a bright light, which turned a dullish red, then white on approaching her window. A rainbow ball of coloured lights would come out of this and hover by her window. It was a small ball, but she felt it was sent to keep tabs on her.

That year on Christmas Day her father died. Her mother was 4 months pregnant with her brother David, who was born 5 months later. They were now very poor and shifted from her Uncle's house on the farm to the suburb where her maternal grandmother lived. Her mother had to go to work and Nain (Welsh for Nanny) had to care for them. She obviously deeply cared for and had very happy memories of this grandmother. She took me to see the small row of Victorian terraced houses, and the house she lived in with her. We went to a rough ground area behind this and sat there. She had asked Ron if he minded very much her going to see her grandmother's house, she had not been there for years.

When we got to this place, she was dismayed to find it completely built over with houses to the cliff edge, which had all been open ground when they had lived there. She sat silent for awhile and then sighed and said "my Nain is long since dead, so why worry" she told me she had had a very happy childhood with kind and loving parents, grandparents and a host of uncles and aunts. So despite her father's death in her 12th year and these traumatic experiences, she had had a secure and happy childhood.

So now, she said, comes the most difficult experience for you to swallow or understand. David was about 5 and she was playing with him on this rough ground at the back. They were not allowed to go round the curve of the bay near the cliffs, but he had wandered off, as she sat down. She then noticed a strange, large insect in the grass. Here I managed to ask if she had not thought it a mechanical device, for she said it started talking to her in a fairly loud clear voice. It said to go and look over the cliffs, at this she noticed David had wandered and yelled to him to return. He came over and she said, "Would you listen to this insect, it is talking to me." When he came the insect continued to talk and told them both to go to the cliffs. (The cliffs I had to look at through binoculars, so they were some distance away). At this her brother ran ahead to the central bowl of the top cliffs, the area drops away several hundred feet to the sea below. He went near the edge to peer at something. She was running towards him, to grab him. When she reached him, she had to forcefully hold him back, it was as though he was compelled to go forward. At this point she saw a dull silver bell-shaped craft about 10/15ft in diameter hovering up and down the cliff face, it would come up to the level of the cliff edge, then go down again. Clutching David's hand, she dragged him home to her grandmother's house. This was the last occasion in her childhood/girlhood that she saw a UFO. I asked if David remembered this. She said yes, she certainly knew he did, but he would not talk about it.

At 21 years of age Jayne was working and going out of an evening with her boyfriend. I interrupted again and asked what she now thought of the talking insect. "Oh, I know now, it could not have been a insect, it must have been something mechanical, a device which could relay voice messages from the craft. That was the first time I thought it was a craft and not a strange sort of caravan, like the ones I saw in the fields."

After this we decided to return to the cove for a break and sit outside the Restaurant. This was where she told me about the experience with her boyfriend which had made her realise she had to face the fact that all that happened in her childhood was not dreams.

On this particular evening when Jayne was 21, she and her boyfriend had driven out in his new car; they were parked by fields, in a lane by the sea. It was a clear evening (I was not told the boyfriend's name). They were talking, when they both noticed a dark rolling mass of mist creeping up the fields towards them.

She felt quite alarmed and suggested they should make for home immediately, but he wanted to stay on. He went on talking as the mist which she was apprehensively watching, crept up and encased the car. At this stage, the boy exclaimed he could see bright lights and they were ships. "What ships" she said, "For God's sake, let's go". He then edged very slowly along the lane, but he kept commenting on the ships with bright lights, but she did not want to look, and felt very irritated with him, for placing themselves in this frightening situation. She kept repeating, "Lets get home quickly". They had gone into this lane on a clear evening at 7.20p.m and by the time they emerged on to the main road it was past 9.00p.m. The lane Ron and I motored on in a few minutes emerging on to the main road. Both Jayne and her boyfriend were aware of the time loss, the boy was very worried about it, as he kept saying "didn't you see the very bright lights". Her recollection is of being vaguely lifted from the car, but not with the boy. The boy was also taken and vaguely recalled this, but he did not go at the same moment as her. The mist had continued thick as they edged their way around, but once on the main road, it was immediately clear.

The following day the boy came over to collect her and show her his car. He was extremely upset that his car bodywork was ruined with many circular rings in threes towards the rear part. They then tried hard to recollect what had happened to them in the two missing hours. They did have vague misty flashes of recollections, but none that they could confirm with words, they seemed to be vaguely at the back of their minds. This was something they continued to do in the following weeks, when sometimes they would recall these flashes. At this point, as we were near a very rocky beach, my dog Mattie elected to wander, and I was constantly being distracted so I am afraid I do not remember this part of the conversation. I was told what some of these flashes of memory were. If I remember the usual abduction scene there were some forms of examination. One thing I recall her saying was that she was taken before The Khan again. This name Khan was one she gave him in her mind, but as she did this first as a small child before the War, it should be remembered there was no television, Star Trek, etc. then at all. I don't think people in the British Isles especially rural Wales concerned themselves much with tales from India then either.

The boyfriend was disturbed, deeply so, for many months after this incident. She again said she had to finally admit to herself the experiences she had had in childhood were real ones and connected to this.

At this stage of the interview Jayne was looking very strained and tired, she said again she was very sorry, she knew we had come a long way and had been very considerate with her, but she could talk no more. She then started walking slowly towards my husband and our car.

So I asked after a bit, if this was the final abduction she had experienced. "No, but she and her boyfriend drifted apart possibly because of it". But then she met her husband, they got married and she had a baby daughter. At the time she and her husband were out walking. They were "abducted into a craft." "I am sorry I am too tired to go into it, it would entail a whole day's telling" and apart from which she did not wish to think of it any more. I asked if her husband recalled this abduction. "Yes, I'm sure he does, but he feels afraid, so the few times I've approached him about it, he has got very rude and says he does not want to discuss UFOs or any other odd things and neither is she to". That is what makes her realise he remembers all right. "It would be useless my taking you to my home, he would only get rude, and he might even be rude to you and I do not want my children (all adults and mostly married) hearing about all this".

116

Had she ever joined a UFO organisation or attended a Meeting? "Yes, a few years ago, I persuaded my elder son to go with me to a UFO Talk in Bristol." She thought they might have been something called Aetherius or BUFORA. "I certainly don't think it could have been BUFORA," I said. "Well, we did not think much of it we got up and left before the end". They talked a lot of nonsense about cattle being mutilated, she said. This her mind utterly rejected.

After this she found John Fuller's book The Interrupted Journey - this had made her feel totally traumatised, as she knew exactly the same things had happened to her husband and herself, apart from the fact that they had been walking and were not in a car. Since, she had decided not to read another UFO book. Learning maybe what someone else had experienced would only confirm hers. She felt she had been Programmed, but not any more. One day if she gained the courage, she might sit down and write it all into a book. Here she said defiantly, "come to think of it, why should you all gain money if you publicise it, I may as well, I suffered enough". This was said in a semi-joking fashion, but then she went back to being serious. She was very agitated about the Voyager probes, the tests NASA were doing, she remembered the things The Khan told her (here she mentioned some of them, as I do not know of them I can't recall what she said). We had sat down again on a stone wall by the sea, but now got up to go to the car "This is it" she said abruptly, "I'm not going to talk any more about this".

We got into the car, she thanked Ron for waiting patiently again, and then she directed us on to the main road. We went some miles before we came to a roundabout, where she told us we should go straight across, but she would like to be dropped off on the grass verge. "I can walk home from here. Thank you for coming. You can tell Jenny Randles, but I will have no names, if you write about it - just put a South Wales woman. No names of places. I have to live here. I'm trusting you now and I don't trust people much" with that she waved and walked quickly away.

We immediately drove a few yards to a lay-by where I proceeded to write 19 pages of notes. I wanted to put all the details down incase I later forgot something. Then my husband and I drove on many miles trying to get B & B in small country villages, we could not find any, as it was almost dusk, we were a bit worried and turned towards the coast again, where we finally found a rather hidden really pretty unknown sea-side small town/village. All except one of the Hotels and B & B were fully booked, this turned out to be very nice, so we relaxed, went to have our dinner in the village Inn taking our dog with us. The hosts couldn't have been nicer, Mattie was given a huge bone, and the host wheeled Ron's wheelchair in. The dinner was good, and we recalled for the first time that day, that it was the 1st June 1991 our 19th wedding anniversary! What an unforgettable day it had been.

In the ensuing months Jayne and I corresponded, she would recall certain points, mainly years and dates more clearly and ask me to rectify them. In essence the narration is correct to the best of her childhood recollections, disjointed and fragmented as they are.

Nevertheless opening up these painful memories upset Jayne considerably, so I suggested it might be therapeutic for her to try and write it all down in a book. Her reaction was vigorous and typical of her "Why not? Why should I let one of these writers get all the money for it, I suffered enough, I may as well earn something, for it". So she started jotting everything spasmodically down. Jayne had to set this aside a long while when she lost her husband and mother within months of each other. Then a while after, it helped her considerably concentrating on her Story.

When I met her again in 1994 she brought a shopping bag full of her writings, wanting me to review them. There was nothing I would like more, but time did not permit. She does not type, so I hope she will eventually get someone to print her Story.

NOTE   The name Khan was something she thought up in childhood, as a name fitting for this exotic-looking being, but she has a vague recollection now that he was referred to as Zoltan.

Royston Jones - South Wales

RJ was 16 in 1944 in the small village of Penywaun in the Aberdare Valley. He was awaiting the bus to take him to work at Cardiff. The sky was a bright blue, when he saw several grey half moon shapes in a line across the sky. Two of these were glowing over a mine's slagheap of ash and rubble. A pit escalator was busily going up and down working on this man-made hill. He could see small ovals of white lights accompanying it.

The line of grey half moons had now formed a full circle, with a black hole in the centre, into which a black cigar was sucked. It seemed like a vortex to him, as eventually only the black hole remained, which then expanded and sucked in the half moons! Gradually this hole faded into the distance. During the duration of this display, everything around RJ seemed to be absolutely still, the birds had ceased to twitter, and there was not another soul in sight, but this is not as mysterious as it may sound, this was after all a small Welsh valley village, so believe me it is quite an event in our areas of rural Wales to see a person walk down the road.

Thereafter RJ started having out of body experiences, even more disconcerting he developed a disturbing ability to see impending disasters and the sorrows of people, an ability he hated having. He told me he married mainly to keep himself in the main stream of Life and his feet firmly on the ground; humbly he admitted not the best of reasons to found a marriage on. Well, he had his family, but this horrible ability persisted. The bonus for him was, that he found he could Faith Heal and therefore he felt he was doing some good. This man came from a humble mining family, who all belonged to the Salvation Army. Whilst he adheres to their way of life, it was interesting to me that his spiritual thinking had developed along quite a different pathway. His is a cosmic awareness, and he had become a deep New Age thinker. All developed from resources from within himself, for he is a rarity, he does not watch television or read newspapers. RJ has quite a sturdy independence of spirit; I have on occasions invited him to attend UFO Conferences with me. He did once, but then politely excused himself, saying he did not want to be influenced by other people's talks, he felt they would no longer be able to channel in so directly to him.

Who are 'they', well there is no doubt in RJ's mind, they are simply Space Intelligences, he is certain they have been contacting him since 1944. Again he feels he was selected, is controlled and monitored by Them, and there is nothing he or any human being can do about this.

By 1987 RJ had numerous physical ailments, and badly needed a hip replacement, his particular job having aggravated some of these complaints. So he went into hospital, being put in a Ward of 4. In the next bed was a Parson, this gentleman confided in the patients that he had foreseen this Ward exactly and his operation proceedings, and he did not like it at all, as it was working out in detail. At this retiring modest RJ for the first time had the courage to tell his fellow patients of his 1944 sighting, which had left him with the uncomfortable ability of being able on occasion, to see into the future.

This was a momentous occasion for RJ, for as he did not read or watch T.V. he had no idea other people had seen UFOs! They simply did not enter into the conversation of people he knew. On the 17th November RJ was wheeled on a trolley to the pre-operation room, where two nurses were to give him an injection. They then saw RJ rise out of his body and go through the ceiling. He saw himself "on a bed of mercury" with a strange thin tall Being rectifying the things that were wrong with his body! They almost fled in terror, and would have if there had not been another patient there. Then they saw the top half of his etheric spirit sink back into his body, as they wheeled him into the Theatre.

In the Operating Theatre RJ was given another injection and put under anaesthetic, when he again felt himself floating out of his body up to the ceiling, from where he watched his entire operation. The Surgeon had some students around him, and he told them "This man has healed himself, only his hip needs replacing".

119

Afterwards, the Surgeon came to the Ward and asked RJ a lot of questions about UFOs; he explained that he had been talking about them under anaesthetic. RJ then dumfounded him and the students, by describing what they did, had said and had stood during his operation.

On one memorable occasion RJ offered to take me to the hospital where all this had taken place, to try to locate the nurses. I regret to say Cardiff s one-way system defeated my husband and myself, and after losing ourselves for what seemed like hours, we were too late to do anything. Numbers of my fellow Ufologists have met RJ; all find him a quiet, dignified very honest little man. Extraordinary as his story is, I personally would never insult him by doubting him, of all the abductees/contactees I've ever met, this man convinces me the most. People who know little about the subject may sneer, they do so out of ignorance.

Here is a man who appears to have had two differing experiences. In the one he seems to have been operated on by an Alien Intelligence who could apparently transfer these rectifications from his ethereal spirit to his corporal body! On the other hand his out of body experiences appear to have only taken place with his etheric self and the nurses saw this happen.

John of Mid-Wales

I always associate Royston Jones in my mind with JT. Both are Welsh, come from the same small community background. They both have the same serene clear approach to life. He is a middle-aged man who has been blind for many years.

When his two daughters were little, he and his wife lived on a houseboat on a canal. One evening his wife had gone out when the boat caught alight. With difficulty, due to the choking smoke JT managed to locate his daughter and carry her out. He says he then saw a UFO, which actually lifted them off the footpath along the canal and gently deposited him where his wife was.

When I suggested he saw this UFO in his mind's eye 'no' he said 'I know I have been blind many years, but I did actually see this craft, and further over the years when I have looked up at the sky, when I have known they are in the vicinity, I see symbols from them'. He told me they communicated with him, although he did not divulge what they said. His wife, who is virtually his eyes, and devoted to him, endorsed everything he said, she sincerely believes he can see these symbols, and over the years they have contacted all walks of people, parson, scientists, astronomers and myself in a vain effort to find out what these symbols mean.

In March 1995 a delegation of 18 people came from all areas of the USA, sponsored by their Government and selected by them to be a Citizen's Ambassador UFO Delegation to England and Ireland; under the leadership of Dr. R. Leo Sprinkle PhD, Counselling Psychologist for Trance Formations Unlimited, Wyoming.

Being of a cynical mind where Governments are concerned, I wondered what Uncle Sam was up to, and if this sincere bunch of people were being duped. I was one of the Ufologists selected to meet this delegation when they came to the North of England, on what was to be for them, a gruelling though pleasurable schedule.

In the course of the evening at an hotel in Manchester, they asked if a blind person had ever reported 'seeing' a UFO. I was quite astonished at this, and related to them the story of JT, saying he desperately wanted to know the meaning of the symbols he saw. Again, to my total amazement, they said they could help him, and he further their studies. They have an Institute in Los Angeles which deals with this issue. Regrettably, I left my copious notes and all their addresses inadvertently in the hotel, and the cleaners threw them away. It has taken a while recontacting these people again, I hope eventually I can put JT in touch with them.

Dirk - of Perth, Australia

I met Dirk when giving a Talk at a Conference in Edinburgh. He was a Lecturer at a Scottish University and a highly intelligent person. Yet in recalling abductions he had been subjected to in childhood, he broke down completely and sobbed.

Born in Perth Western Australia, he had spent his childhood in an outback area where he recalled being abducted between 10,00p.m. and 5.00a.m. one night and on the other occasion in the afternoon between 11.00a.m. and 1.30p.m.

The day following each of these traumatic experiences Dirk felt too ill to attend school. He had skin lesions on the ribs and felt thoroughly exhausted for a long time afterwards.

Dirk does recall impressions of two or three humanoid creatures entering his bedroom. He also has vague recollections of waking up momentarily to see light coloured walls and ceiling with diffused light in them, all round him the textures seemed to have flowing movements, and he was aware he had no pyjamas on.

Dirk's next impression was of being on wet grass and being told to go in and straight to bed. He had childhood impressions of seeing his house from the air and another recollection of being thrown against his window in the afternoon, flinching and finding himself passing right through the glass! When he next recalls sitting in a crouched position on the bedroom floor, and the time is much later than he thought it was.

On one occasion on blowing his nose because it was irritating excessively, a small spherical metallic ball blew out, causing nosebleed.

These are the disturbing fragments of childhood memories that plague this man today. This was the first time he had shared this with anyone. How does he feel today? That was in the 1960s - I do not know the exact year, as I lost touch with him. He did tell me that at one time he flew to New York to visit Budd Hopkins in order to lay these ghosts and accept it had happened and move on.

Janette and Cindy (pseudonyms) - Mid Wales

On Wednesday the 6th March, 1988 Janette and Cindy had heard of a sale of furniture in a Warehouse, which was to take place that evening. They decided to go and look at it. On their way back they were laughing and joking. Foreseeing a UFO appears to be quite common to UFO witnesses, it is a sixth sense just before, people often say they were suddenly compelled to go out of the house or whatever. In this case mother and daughter jokingly said "what if we go round the next bend and we see a UFO, what do we do?' then they giggled. Around the next corner moments later a large colourful craft came from nowhere to the right hand side of the car. It was about 12ft. from them. Cindy was so scared she screamed "Mum, drive as fast as you can, and let us get home" but said Janette, her legs had turned to jelly and she couldn't change gear. The car seemed to have become lifeless, the lights were dimming.

The craft had bright colours of pink, lime green and red which all seemed to mingle together. Eventually their car suddenly spurted into action and she drove as fast as possible to her sister and her husband's house, which was nearer than hers. They only realised afterwards that they were just a few yards from the house, when previously it had been miles away. They were petrified, and her sister and brother-in-law recall the terror on their faces.

Later they reported this to the Police in Newtown, the nearest large town to their village. They had by then realised they had lost 45 minutes of time they could not account for at all, also the miles on the road, they had no recollection of motoring. This left Janette very depressed for months. She then decided to contact various people to see if she could get any help, She wanted to have hypnotic regression, but her daughter would not hear of this, so Janette reluctantly gave up the idea. She was put in touch with me through BUFORA. I think she heard of them on the radio. We had a number of talks on the 'phone, she started reading any UFO books she could get to try and fathom what had happened to them. She arranged to come up and spend a night at my house.

Eventually all these arrangements came to nothing, for her daughter wanted to forget the whole incident, and she felt without her co-operation she could not go ahead with exploring these avenues on her own. They then moved house and I lost touch with her.

Janice - Bexhill-on-Sea, Sussex

Janice's only recollection of ever having seen a UFO occurred in the summer of 1973. At 5.30 p.m. she had come out of Collington Mansions Post Office, Bexhill-on-Sea, where she worked. A colleague used to give her lifts, so she was making her way down the car park, when she looked up to see a huge disc shaped object below cloud level. It had red, green and white lights at its corners, and seemed to hover no more than 90ft off the ground. It was totally silent. She watched this about 10 minutes, looking around to see if there were any other people about, there were none in the car park, although other people in the town saw this. Not only she, but they reported this and were laughed at. So she did not speak of it again.

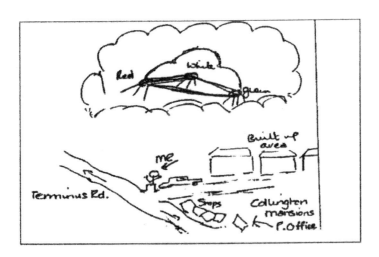

Drawing by Janice recalling her sighting in the Summer of 1973

123

As a child of 14 years Janice had a previous experience of a strange light entering her bedroom. At the time she was with her family at a Butlin's Holiday Camp. She found she could not move, and eventually passed out with fright. In the morning she thought she was having a period, but it stopped, then three months later she started menstruating very heavily, this has always been very irregular for her. During this experience Janice developed a strange line that went from her navel to her pubic bone, this has stayed till fairly recently and is now fading. From then on throughout her child hood she had the same recurring nightmare of a peculiar ugly man entering her bedroom.

In 1976 she had her first daughter, and was told by the mid-wife that this was her second child, because they had found extensive internal tissue damage, which is normally caused by a difficult labour, they also noted the line on her tummy. Fortunately her husband had known her from 16 years of age, he also knew her closest friends who had grown up with her. She was now 21 years. They dismissed the idea from their minds and forgot about it.

Janice's youngest daughter was born in 1978, and she feels today her two girls are having the same experiences as herself, one having been rushed to hospital with a suspected pregnancy in the fallopian tubes, and then no foetus was found. The reason for this could be explainable as a wrong diagnosis by her doctor, for she was only fourteen years of age and a virgin. However this was coupled with the same inexplicable deep line from navel to pubic area that appeared overnight, as had previously happened to her mother.

The youngest daughter too has had the usual unexplainable nosebleeds, and bedroom visitations. More interesting still Janice's husband, to whom she has been happily married since 1974, apparently had an abduction experience in 1975. He is a farmer, and this occurred when he was driving his tractor over a farm field that was owned by his then employer. He suddenly lost time without any recollections of anything outward happening before hand. He had looked at the time, and the next thing he was feeling a bit embarrassed as he was sexually aroused, he looked at his watch and was shocked to see two hours had unaccountably passed, when he had checked a few minutes before; he hurried on in the tractor and hoped his boss would not notice.

Some fifteen years later Janice had a vivid dream in which she saw her husband going across this field in his tractor, then he was abducted and had sperm taken from him, a Being held a conversation with her in which he told her the date, year 1975 and the time this happened. She started talking about this in her sleep, and her husband hearing her woke her up, absolutely amazed at what she was saying, he confirmed that everything she said was true, he had never mentioned the incident to her.

On occasions throughout her life Janice has had feelings of paralysis in bed, only to fall asleep and awake to strange markings and bruises. This type of thing is being reported from almost every country now.

Janice wonders if both she and her daughter were impregnated at 14 years of age, she has a rare Rhesus negative blood group, which neither of her parents had. In recent years her psychic abilities have developed, she sees people's auras, energies and things other people do not appear to see. Like so many people who believe they have been abducted by aliens, Janice feels she has been programmed and there is nothing she can do about it. She feels this has given her the bonus of developing herself more spiritually, she channels all this into work as an Aura Soma Colour Therapist, and hopes she is doing good for people.

This family have shifted from Sussex and now live in another county of Southern England, he is a farmer, she a teacher to handicapped children, the family believe they have been victims of the UFO phenomena, but seem to have accepted it. At any event it does not prevent them from leading normal happy lives in their farmhouse.

Carol - Sussex

Sussex yes, but these two families are unknown to each other, as Janice's family live and own their farm in a totally different county now. These abductions I have personally been involved with are not particular to a county. I am currently in touch with abductees in Sussex, Kent, Gloucestershire, Essex, Suffolk, Wales and Scotland, and sometimes I think they get to hearing about me through the most amazing coincidences, or are they coincidences? Am I also programmed in some way?

Sometimes I think all this is so far fetched, the very practical side of me cries out "it can't be true, they may seem very sincere, regardless they have got to be deluding themselves, if not me deliberately" "OK I think Carol, Janice are educated sophisticated women, they have access to bookshops and libraries, could have read enough about the subject to equate it to themselves". Then along comes a total country bumpkin, whose family do not read, are uneducated, they themselves know nothing about the subject and then they start relating in minute detail what their counterparts in the South are telling me. These details certainly never get into a largely sniggering media, and. only very lately into some of the better UFO magazines. If they were subscribers, we in our closely woven UFO world would soon know.

Then I always remind myself that I had totally inexplicable small footprints in the snow on the extended roof of my house, and the only other living soul who saw them is half

125

blind and over 80 years of age now, my neighbour Mrs Doris Jacques. So I wish someone would take a tape recorder and get her version before it is too late.

In 1977 Carol had been to see a friend, at 7.00p.m. she was returning, when she saw a large orange glow just above some fir trees. It rose up, then came down again as a huge aeroplane came down low going towards it, she thought there would be a collision, but none came, so she drove on home.

Once when Carol and her husband were lying in bed, through the bedroom window they saw an orange glow, accompanied by an engine droning sound. It went on for several hours. As they lived near a railway line, they got up to see if anything else could account for this, then the glow very slowly rose up into the sky. One night for some reason she put on make-up, did her hair and got into bed, that night she saw a yellow ball of light outside the window, which she felt was observing her. At the time her son was 4 years old and she could see lights coming from his bedroom, so got up, drew back the curtains, nothing there, this was in 1976.

They went on a holiday to Sandown, the Isle of Wight. On the ferry she could see the caravan they would be allocated by an open field, and she felt something was going to happen and wanted to turn around and go home. On arrival as in her precognition, the Manager led them to the caravan by the field. On the 2nd week there Carol lay in bed feeling a tingling in her body and unable to move, saw the door handle being turned, after which she fell asleep. In the morning there was a brownish mark on her leg, like she had been branded with a poker. She touched it and felt as though there was something missing in her leg.

Let me go back to Janice talking of her experiences at Bexhill-on-Sea. "Throughout my life, I have often woken up during the early hours of the morning to find my brain awake, but my body under total paralysis. All I can remember on most occasions is a spinning light, a dizzy floating feeling, then total loss of memory.

One morning I found a very sore mark on my arm, a small chunk of skin was missing, this was when I was 11, it went very sore and I had to have it lanced.

The same year they had this holiday on the Isle of Wight, Carol had been out and was given a lift by a lady friend, they saw a huge orange ball arise from the North, which as it went up got larger and larger until it was, enormous. She hurried home to ask her husband to follow it in his car; he did give it a chase until it disappeared over the Coast. Thereafter she repeatedly asked this friend to verify they had seen this, she said "Yes, but she did not wish to discuss it with anyone".

Having seen yellow glows outside their bedroom window and other similar experiences they shifted house in 1978/79 hoping whatever it was would not follow them. When first in this new house, Carol had a strong feeling that a voice was telling her 'they were going now, she was in a safe place'. At this all sorts of frightening events occurred both inside and outside the house! Fire crackers, or what sounded like them would go off near their bedroom window, next morning they would find brown rings the size of a dinner plate on the lawn outside. There would be lights on in their son's bedroom and when they went to check, everything would be normal.

On another occasion Carol was dusting with a duster in one hand and a vase of flowers in the other, as she thought she would put the radio on, the stereo burst out with music, which gave her a terrific start. One morning they awoke to two large bruises, one on her husband's left eyebrow, and Carol had one from her elbow to her right wrist. I said then bruises might have been caused in their sleep, accidentally knocking against each other. She agreed, but said that these bruises they have periodically had, are in such positions as to make this impossible, and further they were a blue/black colour, and did not hurt when touched and just disappear after a week. Whereas normal bruises do hurt and are usually blue/mauve/green.

On this particular occasion this was coupled with their son having a severe nosebleed, his pillow was covered in blood. On another occasion she found her son then only small, was reversed in the bed, with his head neatly on the pillow, and duvet also tucked in neatly. On another occasion a strange guttural 'robotic voice' could be heard talking in their son's bedroom, and he was replying in the same language. Now said Carol their reaction at the time particularly worried them. Any normal parents would go and investigate, and they were normal parents with this their only child. Yet they lay and listened and did not attempt to get up, neither had they felt afraid.

On a morning in 1968, Carol, her husband and son whom they were taking to school, all saw below a very dark overcast sky a very large silver cigar, just over some houses, it had no protrusions. As soon as her son got into the school he told his classmates, only to be ridiculed.

Frequently during the 1980's, the family would awake to an unidentifiable droning sound; it would always be about 1.05a.m. they never got up to see what it was. During this period too, other members of Carol's family wrote to say they had seen UFOs or had UFO-related experiences. Sometimes they would awake to wireless signal sounds just over the roof. Here I must digress and say in 1976 when shifting to a new house during the spring in Bexleyheath, Kent I too was woken up by exactly the same sounds, wondering where the devil they came from. Although I feel that some of the things Carol's family experienced perhaps could be rationally explained away, most were far too numerous and strange and could not, for space does not permit me to list everything that has happened to them over the years and goes on to this day.

Until these things started occurring Carol had only ever read Bermuda Triangle by Charles Berlitz, (Granada Publishing Ltd. 1975) however, as the years went by, being an intelligent educated person, she started to read everything she could find about the paranormal and UFOs, in order to find some answers to what was happening to her family.

1990 was her worst experience. One night they forgot to draw the curtains, and on lying down she saw a little Being with an oval face, pale skin and big bug eyes, just float past the window, next from the other direction, one with a very crinkled looking skin also floated past. She heard a voice saying 'you should not have seen us, it was a mistake' at this she went into a total state of shock. Unable to move, unable to get up and go to the toilet, it took her ages getting over it
In the last few years Simon has become aware 'that ET's are pursuing them'. Having grown up he has invited a couple of girl friends to spend the night. One got very upset and said a Lady with thick lips had appeared, which she drew. The next time I see Carol she is going to show me these. Other visitors have complained of inexplicable happenings.

Carol says she has been told she is a collector of information, she feels she is being monitored and used, but there is nothing much their family can do about it. It has taken a long time coming to terms with it, but again she does feel this has expanded her spiritually, and she has been given the gift of Healing. She has decided to use this for the good of people. It was only after a sterilization operation that the brown mark on her leg gradually faded. Now she feels she has reached mental calm waters; though the bruises and strange markings on her body continue to this day.

Pauline - Queensland, Australia

In 1980 Pauline lived and worked in Bermuda. She was returning home early from work, on her moped motorbike when she saw what she thought was a beautiful sunset. There was a car in front of her, and one at the back. She could see the man in the car at the back also peering at it. As it now occurred to her it was getting closer, and the time was wrong for a sunset.

As it came nearer it became larger and larger. Feeling very afraid, she got off her bike, and stood trembling at the roadside. It was a coastal road with a sea wall, and as this thing approached, she wanted to run to the sea wall to protect herself At this she looked for the car in front, it had gone, and the car to the rear, where the man had also been watching, now seemed to have vanished.

The Object now seemed enormous, it was as large as a very large hotel building, it rotated in a fuzz, coming towards her. The next thing it had swept away sideways, and she was terrified. Pauline picked up her cycle, and wondering why it felt so cold, all her limbs were trembling; she got on and shakily drove home.

On arriving at her home, to her dismay she noted for the first time it was dark, about 10.30p.m. to 11.30 p.m. She could not account for six to seven hours lost. She slept very poorly, but went to work next morning, as she thought she would enquire if anyone else had seen the orange ball in the sky. No one had, she then felt too scared to say anything further. She had felt it was so enormous the whole of the island of Bermuda should have seen it, but none came forward to the newspaper or anything.

Pauline then decided to ring NASA base on Bermuda, asking them what she had seen, and why had it not been put in the newspaper, and why had no one else reported it? The man listened, was non-committal and finally said he could tell her nothing - no comment. Then "I can tell you this Mam, you had a most unusual sighting and experience".

After this Pauline felt very poorly, and had to go into hospital with 'periods' problems, they weren't sure if she had a cyst. She then decided it was time she went back to her homeland Australia, where she came from.

Once home Pauline had many troubles with her periods and womb. Sometimes twice a week, felt paralysed in bed, and could not move at all, when she'd feel a white light pulling at her feet. Two people witnessed this, one a boyfriend living with her at the time. The bed violently shaking would awaken him, and he would see her in a trance like state. The second time Pauline was in a Motel with a girl friend, who was terrified at seeing the same happening. Pauline and her boyfriend loved walking in the countryside of Queensland. When she got to a particular spot, she felt the same magnetic pull, felt violently ill and got sick. Her boyfriend said she looked green, and then she fainted.

Being troubled by these memories Pauline finally went to a professional hypnotist, but all she did was to go into a crouching position, covering her head with her arms, and sobbing, so that the hypnotist had to bring her out of this state, as she was too distressed.

Later Pauline tried a further hypnotic regression from a different angle. The hypnotist on this occasion took her back to her childhood. She recalled at six years of age going to a new school. She decided she did not like it and was leaving. When she got to the front glass door, a man dressed in gold, or maybe he looked radiant, so she thought it was gold, opened the door for her, but said "You can't go home - remember this was your choice, go back into the Class Room". When coming round from this session, she said she wondered if this inferred she had been reincarnated, and she had elected to return to this Life again, and that was what was meant by the 'Man'.

Since living in Wales for the last six years, all these experiences have ceased for Pauline.

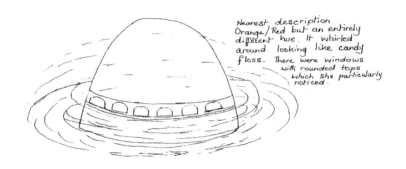

Nearest description Orange/Red but an entirely different hue. It whirled around looking like candy floss. There were windows with rounded tops which she particularly noticed.

Impression of what Pauline saw in Bermuda

Corwen, Clwyd, North Wales abduction

On Friday 17th March 1995 the Denbighshire Press printed an account about a youth from a village called Chirk near Corwen. He had been on his cycle, returning home from seeing his girlfriend, about 8.50p.m. On the A5 between Llangollen and Corwen, there are high-forested mountains, rising steeply from the road. At one point there is a distinctive scree, with a maintenance hut or building just below it on the road, above all this is a reservoir. It was here the youth stopped to watch a long strange craft descending from the top and along the scree down to the road. It was what he could only describe as a long car, which when it hit the road, let off sparks in the air. It then came along the right hand side of the road below the forested area, and stopped opposite him where he was standing at the lay-by.

There were eight Beings in this of varying heights 6ft 6inches to 5ft 7inches. They had different types of faces as humans do. Large foreheads, smaller or larger noses, thicker lips etc. They were dressed in leather thigh-length jackets. From the excellent drawings the youth did, they all looked middle-aged, to elderly.

Two Beings got out and approached him and spoke to him in their own language, but it seemed to be conveyed to him that they had lost somebody, and required his help to locate him.

The events after this were hazy for the youth, at one stage he seemed to think the whole 'long car' went up into the woods in the mountain above the road. The trees are densely packed there, so did it shrink to nothing in order to achieve this? The young man then found himself and his cycle 50 yards further along the road, and he noted it was 10.30p.m. he was feeling shaken and went into Llangollen to phone his mother. He had lost 1 hour 50 minutes he could not account for. This occurred in September 1994.

I do not get this local newspaper, so the first I heard of it was through The Cheshire UFO Studies Group. Eric Morris is a psychiatric nurse, and his Group members and he thoroughly investigated the case. They felt that as this youth was an unsophisticated village boy he would not have invented such a story. He did not refer to these Beings as Aliens, but as strange men. Later at one of our three monthly Social Evenings, Eric came and gave the Welsh Federation of Independent Ufologists, North Wales branch a full account of what transpired.

Ron Lalek one of the Investigators, now our WFIU representative in Flintshire, discussed this case with me in depth. He subsequently saw this youth on a number of occasions, and believes this did happen to him and thought I should write about it.

Gary Rowe, long time researcher and co-founder with me of the Welsh Federation, and I felt peeved that we had not been invited at the onset to investigate this with the Cheshire Group, for they had come over the border to visit this young man. Since the advent of the Internet, more UFO Conferences in major cities of Britain, and glossy UFO Magazines on bookstalls, Ufologists all over Britain have more access to other county cases. It should still be a courtesy to contact the local Investigators and inform them of what has occurred in their own backyard, and offer to conduct the investigation with them. Even if the witness or abductee do not wish to see more than the initial person contacted, the courtesy to inform the local investigator should be extended before rather than after the event.

The majority of abductees who have approached me I have met at Alan Hilton's Kent UFO weekends; people from all over Britain attend them. For every one of the cases that I have written about, there are several more I made no notes on. Alan and I just tried to assist these people. It is not always possible to contact the county investigators, but the effort should be made.

NOTE: Credit - Ron Lalek, Eric Morris and Members of the British UFO Studies Centre, Cheshire.

Amongst all these cases I have written about and know of personally, and these are by no means all of them, there is not one single one that has an independent witness to an abduction. Indeed other members of a family of an abductee will say they saw them asleep, and nothing happened. They may have been asleep themselves when the abduction was supposed to have taken place. One notable exception was a relatively recent case given us by Budd Hopkins professional painter and sculptor in New York, who has for years endeavoured to help American abductees at his Studio, by hypnosis methods and self-help abductee group meetings.

At a Sheffield Conference organised by Philip Mantle and BUFORA in 1991, I listened totally fascinated to Budd Hopkins, telling us about Linda, a Lower East Side Manhattan, New Yorker who had been abducted from her high-rise apartment in the small hours of the morning of 30th November 1989. Linda in her early forties said she had been lying in bed by her sleeping husband, when she opened her eyes to see a small grey-skinned creature standing by her bed. She tried to awake her husband, could not, and then threw a pillow at the creature. Then her limbs became numb and within minutes she had lost consciousness. Later with Bud's regressive hypnosis Linda was able to recall that several little greys had floated her out of the window upwards in a blue beam of light into a saucer shaped UFO. Later Linda was floated back, landing in bed with a thump.

Fifteen months later in February 1991, Bud received a letter from two men calling themselves Richard and Dan, who claimed to be Police Officers, who saw the kidnapping of Linda and the oval UFO fly over FDR Drive, then plunge into East River by Brooklyn Bridge. Later they said they were Security Agents guarding the then United Nations Secretary General Javier Perez de Cuellar.

In November 1989 a retired telephone operator from Putnam County, New York had written to tell Bud that she had also seen Linda being floated out in her white nightgown, together with some small figures in a blue beam of light to the hovering oval shaped UFO. She had been in her car on Brooklyn Bridge, and there were several cars there at the time which all stopped, some of the motorists ran from them in terror. She herself had been very frightened. The light from the Spacecraft had been so garish, that she wondered that thousands more had not witnessed it.

The Slides Budd Hopkins showed us were really impressive. So that I was quite amazed and disappointed, when my fellow British buffs seemed to hardly attach any significance or importance to this incredible case.

I had a brief conversation in the foyer with Budd Hopkins afterwards, and felt he looked equally bemused at this low key British reaction to what he felt should be a world shattering case, and a break through for Ufology, for this was the first abduction case, which other witnesses had testified to seeing. I think Bud sensed the atmosphere of apathy to this for he seemed to withdrawn into himself. I cannot recall much being written about this extraordinary case by our British UFO magazines, later Jim Schnabel wrote a book 'Dark White' and then the Sunday supplements here made much of the Linda case.

At the same Conference too, a very respectable looking and/speaking English Doctor from a Scandinavian country spoke up and was by-passed. She said she had also been abducted into an alien craft, and been medically examined. Again I was amazed at the West Yorkshire Group and BUFORA organisers. I do not think we have ever had a case of a Doctor being abducted; we could have learnt perhaps valuable points from her, yet they all seemed to totally ignore her.

Subsequently, the British UFO fraternity has welcomed Bud Hopkins to speak a number of times at the hugely popular Conferences UFO Magazine – Graham W Birdsall and his family have organized each year at Leeds for the general public.

I do not think we can afford to sit on the fence any longer. This is not just an American scenario, there is a frightening build-up of Abductions from all over the world. My own abductees have totally varying lives and lifestyles. Yet the same thread of evidence runs through all their stories. Most of them are people I have got to know over years, they place their trust in me. They know they have had real physical traumatic experiences, no matter what other people may like to theorise.

So what are we in Ufology going to do about this? I suggest the only way forward is to realise this full force of evidence gives a basis for a reality. We should combine to try and convince our medical profession at least about the validity of this Reality. Abductees are often treated incorrectly by them for physical ills after an abduction, thereby adding to their distress. We must make an all out effort through T.V., Radio, articles and books to try and convince medical people. The more professionals we get interested the sooner the public at large will accept. There is nothing more powerful than People Power.

I am acquainted with a lady in Tunbridge Wells, Kent whose 17-year-old daughter went missing from her bedroom one night 3 years ago. She noted the back door was wide open on getting up herself in the middle of the night. She got her son up and they went looking for the girl and found her muddied and crumpled up lying in the field totally distressed and traumatised. Bringing her in they had to sit on the sofa for the remainder of the night, as she sobbed out a distressing account of being kidnapped by Aliens who took her out and genetically engineered and raped her.

Not for this victim an obliterating time lapse, she remembered in full her distressing ordeal, as her family tried to grasp what has happened to her. At night the whole family are afraid to go to bed now, and the girl used to beg them to chain her to the bed. For a long time she had all sorts of distressing physical symptoms of her ordeal. Eventually she decided she had to leave that house and build up a new life elsewhere.

Whilst more than three quarters of the population take these frightening bizarre abductions as a laughable fantasy, who in authority is there to help them? As on the 3rd February 1996 at 4.30p.m. on BBC 2 a programme with Esther Rantzen went out, Maria Ward, a well-known abductee was invited to take part. She was disgracefully humiliated and derided by this famous person who is so compassionate with children, yet did not have the sensitivity to see that Maria too is a victim of rape. Why did not Esther trouble herself to read up something about the UFO phenomenon before upsetting this lady so publicly without allowing her any redress?

Some readers might think - victim of what? What is this abduction scenario? Is it a reality, as we know it? I know some UFOs are a reality as we know it in our three-dimensional world, because I have seen them. I have not seen aliens, but I believe I have seen the physical traces of them, with the footprints I had on my roof on the 17th January 1977. What about the two to three bedroom apparitions I have written about? In my mind I liken them to laser beamed holograms, that makes for much more comfortable thinking. Mankind after all has the technology now to make pretty patterns with lazer beams on clouds, so why not one step further by a more advanced technology than ours to bedroom visitations?

So can these 'holograms' then kidnap people from their beds? Surely not. So what about the theory that if these Beings are on another dimensional level to us they are only able to pluck our etheric spirits from our bodies in some way? And so only our minds, intellects, etheric selves have this experience? Apparently, alien technology and intellects then have the ability to transfer changes and scraps of physical evidence such as scars and bruises to our corporal body as seemed the case with RJ at Cardiff Too far fetched? UFO researchers, often armchair ones, talk grandly of metaphysics. What are metaphysics, the Dictionary defines the word as theoretical philosophy, abstract theory.

So O.K. with the above I'm going into metaphysics. What of mental aberrations, so beloved by the sceptics? We can't all be qualified psychiatrists like Professor John E. Mack. In the absence of these medical professions, we in the UFO fraternity are aware of this and do band together over abduction cases. We consult psychiatric nurses in our numbers, and to the best of our ability try to ascertain the person is not suffering from mental illness. Some sadly are, but the overall majority are sane, sensible ordinary people who have had an experience, or experiences that neither they, I nor anybody else can equate with.

The majority of the people I meet who have these experiences are deeply affected for years after, maybe all their lives, others seem to use it as a spiritually uplifting experience, after the initial shock and trauma wears off. None that I have come across here in Britain, have gone on to devote 38 years to analysing and investigating other peoples experiences as I have after experiencing something myself. In 1995 when I met Marie Ward it was a pleasure to realise that she in her own way, is doing, what I have for so many years. Far from being in the majority, it is a lonely path we tread, and when one meets a fellow traveller, what a joy and relief it is. Age does not come into this, for the spirit never grows old, if you do not let it.

Those few amongst our researchers, who have undertaken to help abductees, are in the role of Counsellor. We listen, try to help and above all give a believing support. Of course there are loopholes in their stories, I having been in the business of UFO investigating the best part of 38 years would more readily pick them out than the cynic reading this. Sometimes I take a perverse pleasure in picking out the naiveté of Hopkins, Sprinkle and Mack, all men more qualified than I, but when it boils down we are all exploring an unknown frontier in which we are all amateurs, we are counsellors not Inquisitors.

Numbers of UFO researchers, particularly in America, now accept that people from all over the world, many from Third World countries, whose minds are uninfluenced by books, magazines, T.V., radio or electrical fields and impulses are all relating the same type of craft and humanoids as seen in the USA, UK or Europe. Can aeroplanes flying 30,000 + feet in the atmosphere be affected by electrical impulses? And do the air pilots who report near collisions with UFOs hallucinate? There are many more pilots reporting these to us privately, than ever manage to get into the newspapers. They are responsible for the lives of 200 to over 400 passengers. Small wonder nothing under the sun induces me to enter an aeroplane! Seriously though, whilst I agree that electrical impulses can affect human brain wave patterns, we are after all composed of electrical impulses, everybody having the same hallucinations is a theory full of as many holes as a colander.

135

To me it is far more logical to suppose that as our Milky Way galaxy alone is composed of 2.50 billion stars in an encompassing Universe that our best brains and mathematicians calculate has at least 100 billion inhabited galaxies! Why are there humans conceited enough to imagine our middle-aged Sun has the only inhabited planet revolving around it? Our third, small planet is insignificant in our own Universe. Mathematically we should at least conclude that at least some of these billions of planets have reached a stage of interstellar exploration and could be coming to this Earth. Have you ever looked into people's faces to note we have eyes, nose, mouth, foreheads, and hair yet each of us is recognisably different - unique? So too must each and every planet be unique and worth exploring. It is only in the last few years that in Britain we have begun to speculate that these Beings may not be of our composition and dimension, this is something beyond the thinking of the majority of people. People who have gone into esoteric and New Age thinking, those of the Buddhist and Hindu religions and some primitive societies who have never lost their sixth sense, have for aeons realised there are higher levels of consciousness and dimensions. I have indeed investigated cases where I have pondered, that these other dimensional Beings are able to take our etheric selves out of our bodies from bedroom visitations or even certain abductions out in the open, and it is this part of one's being that has these abduction experiences. In other cases these are quite definitely physical experiences where people return with physical symptoms of having been abused. Yet again the experience seems to be conducted on both levels. Whichever way, it is reality, for we cannot as human beings separate our etheric selves/intellects until the day we die. People might argue that mystics and clairvoyants can, I am referring to the ordinary men and women all over the world, who until that moment were no different from anybody else.

A few years ago, there was a programme, on television, possibly BBC 1, of Mark Tully's. He is the BBC correspondent in India, and I do try to video all his programmes, particularly Travel. This was about the Indian monsoon, and the effect the rains had on the lives of Indians from the Bengal estuary to up into the mighty Himalayas, to remote Bangla Desh high areas, Arunchal Pradesh to Bhutan. All extremely difficult places to get into and travel. India is to these people the Moon, and other countries simply do not exist, except perhaps Outer Mongolia and parts of remote China. For me it was totally fascinating, and I have regretted forever more that I did not video it, as right in the middle was an unexpected gem. The Head Man in a village was complaining to Mark Tully in Hindustani that when they were working in the rice fields, space craft came down and shot beams at them, which burnt their skin, could he not complain to the Indian Government about it, and get them to do something! The Imperturbable Mark Tully carried on as though this was of no importance, beyond a momentary amusement; no doubt it was just that to him, for he possibly does not believe UFOs exist.

Another occasion in November 1990 BBC2 presented a travel T.V. programme 'The Last African Flying Boat' by Alexander Frater. Unfortunately I missed this but read his graphic account in The Independent or Guardian about Africa's forgotten island Ilha de Mozambique, he talks of "the total devastation caused by the civil war". In their semi-derelict Pousada Hotel he is talking to the interpreter Juan, when an undernourished youth walked in, he calls him and says "look at this fellow's arm. By the elbow there is a burn. Can you see it? He got that last night from a UFO. Recently it has been paying us visits, beaming down a ray that burns the skin. I can show you other people with similar afflictions. The UFO is about 50 metres across. It is green and very pretty, like a big firework and quite silent. It hovered over the island for a minute or two then vanished in a flash of green flame". 'How many refugees are there here?' I asked. "Ten thousand perhaps. A 1,000 have come in the past two weeks alone". 'Where do they get their food?' He shrugged, "Where they can. At low tide they find shellfish, or seaweed. Sometimes there is rice. There are plants they can cook, and the bats are edible".

Personally, I have been in a bloody civil war, I have been starving, you can't sleep because your stomach is touching the back of you, and your bones painfully protrude into the mattress, that is if you are lying on one, at the time we didn't have such a luxury, and what is your last waking and imagined thought? I assure you food, food and food - nought else.

What of the following, one of many in remote places related by Gordon Creighton in Flying Saucer Review over decades, and also by other writers.

The Rev. Norman E. G. Cruttwell, MA made these reports from the island of New Guinea. There were 79 in all, many equally as fantastic as those of Father W. V. Gill and his missionary station at Boianai, New Guinea. The UFO visited this station on three occasions. Altogether there were 5 Papuan teachers, 3 medical assistants, Father Gill and 25 other Papuans living on the station. None of these people with the exception of the European priest knew about 'flying saucers'. The sightings occurred between the 26-28th June 1959 at round about 6.00p.m. in the evening. The craft was about 300ft. above them.

On Saturday the 27th June 1959 one of the medical assistants called Father Gill and several others, the sun had not set and it was quite light. There were two smaller UFOs above the hills behind stationary, and this larger one came overhead, sufficiently low for them to see four human figures near the centre deck (see drawing). 3 seemed to be doing something but the fourth looked down at them. Father Gill raised his arm and waved, to their surprise the four Beings responded and waved back. As it began to get dark, one of them went to fetch torches, and they directed a series of flashes at the

UFO, this seemed to be acknowledged by the Object wavering back and forth, sideways like a pendulum. Then it seemed the Object got bigger, as it was coming towards them. Then the Beings went in, two returned later to continue what they were doing, and the priest and mission people dispersed for dinner, then Church for Evensong. The rough estimate for the Object was 35ft in diameter 20ft high and the Beings possibly 6ft. They continued to see UFOs the following day and they were also seen at Giwa, Baniara and Sideia[11] (FSR Special Issue No.4 August 1971).

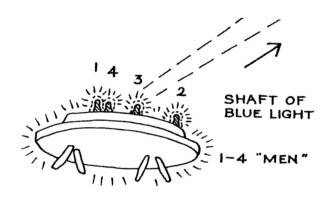

Object with "men" as it appeared over Boianai on July 26, 1959.
Tracing of drawing by the Revd. W. B. Gill

There is also another fascinating report from a remote area on the Chinese/Tibetan boarder at Phewa Tal in the Himalayas. Stephen Gill and Roddy Baird English students were working with Tibetan refugees at Kathmandu. They had taken time off to explore and gone to this remote lake that afternoon to swim, 18th April 1972. About 45 minutes before sunset, after their swim, they were drying off and standing by the lake edge they saw a swarm of dots, then more came and performed an aerial ballet. They debated on whether they could be birds, it was too far away for bees. Gradually these dots solidified and turned to conventional saucer shapes, seen at various angles. They had a Kodak camera with them, so took photos. As an Object came nearer, it developed a smoke ring, which faded after seconds. Then they would see another aerial ballet in another section of the sky. They managed with difficulty to take a few photos. The following day they returned to the Lake but saw nothing, then they returned to Kathmandu. Eventually when they returned to England, they arranged to meet Charles Bowen and permitted him to re-print the photos for F.S.R. (Vol. 19 No. 4 July-August 1973).

All the foregoing is in argument against people who persist in saying all these incidents relate to electrical impulses affecting brain wave patterns, which bring on hallucinations of close sightings of UFOs and abductions.

How is it possible for people from such differing cultures from all over the world, even in remote areas untouched by Western thinking, to have the same hallucinations? This is simply not feasible. In my view this theory falls down and is totally flawed because of this factor.

I would recommend that anyone coming into Ufology to research today, should beg borrow and if possible buy, back numbers of this our most prodigious magazine, it first came out in 1954, and for decades Gordon Creighton the Editor faithfully recorded and translated reports from all over the world. How many people can read, write and converse in about 20 different languages? He was a terrific asset to Ufology and unfortunately as so often happens, he is far more appreciated in other countries than he is in his own. His son, Phillip Creighton, has taken over the Editorship of FSR since his death in 2003.

There is little point in researching locally, and seeing this only as a localised issue, neither can you research without knowing about the history of your subject, and there are no better text books than FSR.

AUTHOR's NOTE:

The chance of a UFO colliding with a commercial plane is hardly likely. If they come close to a jet, it is because they may be curious and wish to be seen. Their craft are so much in advance of ours there is scarcely any remote chance of a collision.

NOTES -

1. *Intruders Foundation- Contact - Budd Hopkins, P.O.Box 30223, New York NY 10011 U.S.A*
   Budd Hopkins Witnessed. Pocket Books 1996
       Missing Time
       Intruders

2. *Whitney Streiber - Communion Arrow Books 1987. Transformation Arrow Books 1986*

3. *R.Leo Sprinkle PhD Counseling Psychologist*
   406 1/2 21st Street,Laramie WY 82070 U.S.A

4. *John E. Mack Abduction . Simon & Schuster London, England, U.K. 1994*

5. *Philip Mantle & Carl Nagaitis - Without Consent Ringpull Press Ltd. Cheshire, England, U.K. 1994*

6. *Elsie Oakensen - One Step Beyond. Into the Unknown - Or is it? Regency Press London, U.K. & New York) Ltd.*

7. *Ken Philips Witness Support Group*
   Contact James Millen, 84 Dyers Lane, Putney, London SW15 6JU, England, UK

8. *Breaks - in the 19th century so called in the Llyn Peninsular, probably a horse drawn carriage, similar to a post chase. The annual Fair Mrs Williams refers to, in fact took place every six months (page 39)*

9. *The hamlet of Saron seems to no longer be in existence (page 40)*

10. *The wartime RAF airfield, now derelict is 3. 1/2 miles from the town of Pwllhelli and Whispering Sands beach 7 miles across the Llŷn Peninsular from there (page 39)*

11. *A full account of this is in Flying Saucer Review (Special Issue No. 4 August 1971) P.O. Box 162 High Wycombe, Bucks HP13 5DZ, England, U.K. – for back issues.*

CHAPTER 4

A HISTORY OF THE UFO PHENOMENON & UFOLOGY

The present day UFO organisations came into being just after the 24th June 1947. That day an American commercial pilot Kenneth Arnold was asked to locate wreckage of a C-46 Marine transporter in the Cascade Mountains of Washington Province. He decided to fly in the vicinity of Mount Rainer, which is about 10,000 ft. Whilst he was trying to locate the wreckage nine metallic objects passed his plane. With the backdrop of snow and sunny clear skies, he could see them distinctly, their flight was like speedboats on rough water, and they emitted bright blue-white flashes from the reflection of the sun. When landing at Pendleton, Oregon he estimated they had passed at 1,350 miles per hour, a then unbelievable speed. Within a day all the newspapers of the world had headlined the story of 'flying saucers', a cliché coined by the journalists[1].

This gave a great number of people around the world the courage to report their own sightings from previous years. Former American and German World War II pilots recalled the unexplained ovals of intense white lights that had followed their fighter planes in battle, which they had nicknamed Foo fighters each side thinking the other had invented them.

So inevitably small bands of people in America, Britain and Europe formed Flying Saucer Clubs to chase the latest UFO reports. Generally speaking these first Ufologists were uncritical and eagerly awaited dramatic developments that man was being visited from other worlds.

At the time there was the Cuban crisis, Fidel Castro and other world incidents which were virtually precipitating us into a 3rd World War. It seems initially the governments of the day decided on a strict clamp down, anyone having the audacity to report a flying saucer was to be ridiculed. Someone reporting a strange object in the sky could certainly have caused hasty Military reaction. Within a few years this had the desired effect with the world media. 'You can fool some of the people some of the time, but not all the people all of the time'. For whether the Governments liked it or not, and they didn't - the UFOs kept on coming! During those years the best of reports came from France, there were such exceptional investigators there, Aime Michael, the scientist Dr Pierre Guerin and Jacques Vallee.

In Britain the first UFO investigation group was formed as the British Flying Saucer Bureau in 1953,the president was Mr Graham Knewstub. By 1955 they were producing an interesting little booklet -Flying Saucer News, Editor Richard Hughes. Price 1 shilling 6 pence. It wasn't until 1962 that they formed a federation of UK groups, which eventually lead to BUFORA being formed, with Mr Knewstub as the 1st President[2].

The Earl of Clancarty, Brinsley le Poer Trench firstly founded the International Sky Scouts in 1964. He was feted by the Japanese Cosmic Brotherhood Association, which shows by now the movement had spread all over the world. Apparently the Baden Powell organisation objected to the title, so this became Contact International based at Oxford, which produces our excellent little magazine Awareness. I was amongst the first members in 1967 and have been an Investigator and Representative for them since 1971. Bernard Delair the President, over 40 years has produced statistics for UFOs. At one time we had 34 member countries, but all Groups and Organisations are down on membership. A few stalwarts keep these afloat. In Contact our Administrative Officers Geoff Ambler, Francis Copeland, Mike Soper and Bill Foley have done for decades.

In the Wales Federation of Independent Ufologists which I co-founded with Gary Rowe in 1993, Mike Orton, John Roberts, Maureen Pumford, Ron Lalek, Richard Foxhall, Richard Alexander, Gary and I keep the WFIU in existence at the present time.

Since these Organisations were founded a new type of Ufologist has been born, not only here but also in America, Australia, New Zealand, France, Brazil, in fact everywhere. They are people who carefully evaluate, discuss and study the phenomena. We have people in all walks of life, Historians, Aircraft Designers, pilots, psychologists, archaeologists astronomers, police, nurses, but unfortunately, hardly any Doctors, of course people in ordinary jobs, also unemployed people. All are welcome if they apply sensible logics and are prepared to be methodical and undertake a hell of a lot of paper work! Three quarters of an Investigators job is this, not chasing after a report of little green men! The popular press idea is that we do. Yes, we do increasingly get CE4 cases (Close Encounters such as abductions). Overall the majority of UFO reports come from ordinary people genuinely puzzled by what they've seen and wanting to make sense of it, hoaxes are infinitesimal. Generally too, after careful research we can turn these UFO reports into identifiable objects, such as dirigibles, weather balloons, sea maroons, even the sun, moon and stars of higher magnitude seen through differing atmospheric conditions. Sometimes this is a disappointment or alternatively a relief to the witnesses.

Our British pioneer researcher was Harold Wilkins a scholarly historian of Bexleyheath, Kent. His son Martin became a family friend after his father's death in

1955. Other early British researchers were Waverley Gavin, a former War air pilot and first Editor of Flying Saucer Review (Feb.1955). Christian 'Tim' O'Brien archeologist, Desmond Leslie a distant cousin of the Queen, Leonard Cramp aero dynamics engineer and Alan Watts physicist. There are no doubt others whose names I have missed out. It is their research through The British Library & Archives, private British, Vatican & Egyptian Museums, medieval monastic records, and also their liaison with pioneer American researchers that has brought to light some of the history I can but briefly outline.

The 1st known record of UFOs is from the Vatican Museum, the Royal Annals of the Pharaoh Thutmosis III (circa 1504-1450 B.C.). "In the year 22, the 3rd month of winter, the sixth hour of the day the scribes of the house of life saw a circle of fire in the sky...." They went to the Pharach, and within a few days this sighting turned to several seen for a few days, not only a large assembly of people, but the army and the king watched these, they were described as whole fleets of craft ablaze with lights 'spitting fire' an apt description for the then unknown or dreamt of electricity with revolving lights[3].

In 329 Alexander the Great leading his Army through Asia Minor, had a great shining craft swoop down out of the sky, scattering and dividing his long column of terrified soldiers[4].

The great historians of the 3rd and 4th century before Christ such as Aristotle, Pliny, and Seneca, then Charlemagne, St Bede and other medieval monks throughout the ages carefully chronicled strange craft seen in the skies some at really close quarters, there are numerous references to 'air ships' coming to this Earth, these generally received short shrift and in some recorded instances the occupants were cruelly put to death. Of course no doubt since those ancient times, space Beings who came here have advanced too, now they immobilise humans with gun rays and abduct them for medical examinations, the boot is on the other foot!

These craft from historical times seem to be identical with the UFOs reported by people today, though the descriptions are termed in the medium of the day. To go even further back in time, the bible is peppered with UFO reports if you read them carefully and in the light of our present day knowledge. There are ancient Hindu Sanskrit writings known as Drona Purva[5], in which there are terrible air battles related, destroying the Vrishnis and Andhakas races.

In the present times there are records of African, American and Latin Americans farmers shooting at UFOs that have hovered over their land. So it seems the Universe is peopled with Beings that are much the same as us humans, bad, good, and indifferent. There are many tales aching to be retold, for many of the books they come from, are out of print and impossible for newcomers to Ufology to obtain. I could fill a book with these 2nd, 3rd and 4th hand accounts, and they make very interesting reading. However, I do have enough 1st hand knowledge and information which I feel needs telling. This book is mainly autobiographical and relates my own research and findings, as said in the introduction.

For this chapter, I give some of these records and tales that have stayed in my mind.

776 AD in the Annales Laurissenses by Drake. The Saxons were attacking a fortress full of Christians, who lived within the castle, which had a Church. All beheld the likeness of two large shields reddish in colour in the sky and immediately the pagans were thrown in confusion and fled in terror.

During the reign of Charlemagne, Emperor of France (742-814 A.D.) Spacecraft took away people of this Earth to show them their wonders. In his Emperor's History the Comte de Gabails says 'Aeriel peoples were seen in the air, sometimes on wonderfully constructed aerial ships whose flying squadrons roved at will'. When these unfortunate abductees were returned to Earth, the populace would assume they were Space people or sorcerers and torture them to death. Both Charlemagne and his successor Louis the Debonair decreed terrible penalties for these 'tyrants of the air'.

Amongst many instances 3 men and a woman were returned to Lyons and the entire city gathered around them crying they were magicians sent by Grimaldus, Duke of Beneventum, Charlemagne's enemy. The abductees vainly endeavoured to explain, but were thrown on a fire. At the last moment Agobard Bishop of Lyons rescued them, giving them a fair hearing, he fortunately decided they *had been abducted.* A man about 2000 years ahead of his time! Which Bishop in our present day would give credence to an Abductee's plight?

In 1207 A.D. A man was seen to emerge from a air ship whose anchor was caught in a pile of stones near the city of Bristol, wrote Gervase of Tilbury, the man freed the anchor suddenly he grasped his neck, and gasped for air, and fell dying to the earth, watched by a crowd of curious people. Gervase of Tilbury recounts that the anchor that was cut free was taken and made into an iron grill for the doors of a basilica, for the public to look at, but no mention is made of the body.[6]

Gervase of Tilbury circa 1200 A.D., was a scholar in the reign of King John of England, he was said to be a relative of the Earl of Salisbury. He was an adventurer and traveller, and become a favourite at the Court of Emperor Otto 1V,under whose patronage he wrote these interesting titbits of history and geography, an encyclopaedia titled Otto Imperiala. [7]

Unfortunately I notice that in almost every book on UFOs different versions of Gervase writings are given. I rather favour the one that puts the locality in a churchyard at Gravesend, Kent, by the Thames Estuary. It would be wonderful if some ancient Church there unearthed a long forgotten Parish Box record of this event in indecipherable olde English, which could confirm this. Surely there is no smoke without fire. In the Gravesend account a man comes down from the air ship, but 'died stifled in our gross air, as a shipwrecked mariner would be in the sea'. The air ship sailed away, leaving her anchor flukes hitched unto the church door, so they forged iron bands for it, so that it is there for all men to see. This was vandalised at the fall of the Roman Empire.

1290 A.D. Byland Abbey, Yorkshire, England.

This document came to light in the mid-1950's in a muniments room at Ampleforth near York possibly by Roger Bacon who recorded 'signs portents in monastic annals' and wrote Opus Majus which dealt with experimental science and prospective, for which rulers and theologians tried him and cast him in jail for 14 years. He continued to write during his incarceration and when freed died in 1294.

This record is incomplete; the monks of Begeland Monastery were sitting down to say grace at their table in the refectory on the feast of St. Simon and St. Jude, when a brother monk Joannes rushed in to call them out to behold an awful thing, a nearly circular object of silvery appearance, not unlike a discus flying slowly above them, which excited the greatest terror in them all. The Abbot Dom Henricus cried out that Wilfred who had provided the sheep for the feast, was a fornicator of women ......[8].

The Fate magazine of March 1958 carried a translation of a 13th century record, again how accurate? This appears to have taken place in Ireland at Cloena. 'One Sunday whilst the population were at Church hearing Mass, an anchor was dropped from the sky as if thrown from a ship, for a rope was attached to it, one of the flukes from the anchor caught in the arch of the church door. The people rushed out, and saw a ship with men in it, one came down the rope to release the anchor, and tried to loosen it, but the people rushed forward and seized him. Then the Bishop present forbade them to hold the man, saying it would prove fatal, as it would be as if they were holding his head under water. As soon as the man was released, he scrambled up the rope, and then the crew cut it and it sailed away out of sight.

There is a similar type of record in mid-America in the late 1800's but this Being died and was given a Christian burial by the local Sheriff. There is periodic interest in this and Ufologists research archives and try to locate this grave in the Church yard.[9]

So these stories go on through the 14th, 15th, 16th, 17th century to Jonathan Swift, the famous Irish 18th century writer. He knew that the Martian satellites Phobos and Deimos were artificial. He knew their distance from Mars and periods of rotation and he published this in Gulliver's Travels in 1726.

Some 175 years later Asaph Hall at the United States Naval Observatory observed and recorded data almost identical to Swift's. In 1959 a Russian scientist Dr.L.Shkolovsky[10] announced that Mars two moons were artificial. There could be no explanation for them in nature.

Deimos is about 5 miles in diameter and Phobos 10 miles. The later is approx: 5,800 miles from Mars and takes 7 hours 39 mins. to orbit it. Deimos is 14,600 miles and its orbit lasts an Earth day, plus 6 hours and 18 mins. Apparently Phobos has deviated from its orbit 2½ degrees in a few decades and speeded up its movement getting closer to Mars.

It would seem that Jonathan Swift was abducted to a satellite above our Earth, or taken to Mars and fearing he would be put into a bath of boiling water, the senseless cure for madness in the 17th and 18th centuries, he turned his experiences into fairy tales, writing Lilliput Land and Gulliver's Travels based on them. How else did Swift gain the 20th century knowledge that has been conclusively confirmed by the American Voyager probes, when they sent back enhanced photos of Phobos and Deimos, when the Americans probe went to Mars.

There was a very interesting report in the late 1980's when Russia first sent Space probes, of an enormous defunct Space Station about 4 to 5 miles above our atmosphere, which is still circling this Planet. Our Press has never resurfaced this story, one wonders why? And of course no power on Earth would admit to it being *an occupied Space Station,* but I have wondered since if some of the UFOs people see emanate from it. And was this in fact Jonathan Swift's Lilliput Land?

People are fond of declaring 'why don't astronomers report UFO's'. Numbers of the first reports came from astronomical observatories.

In 1762 two Observatories in Switzerland saw a huge spindle-shaped Object cross the sun, and at Lausanne a Monsieur de Rostan observed an enormous craft nearly every day for a month, he managed to photograph it and sent this to the Academy of Sciences of Paris. It was the first known photograph taken of a UFO.

Again in 1777 a French astronomer Charles Messier saw a number of dark objects cross the sky. In 1883 an astronomer called Bonilla at an Observatory in Mexico saw circular objects crossing the sun, he managed to take a photograph.[11]

Professor Clyde W.Tombaugh, the astronomer, who discovered the planet Pluto in 1930, was sitting in his garden one clear evening, enjoying the air with his wife and mother-in-law at Las Crucas, New Mexico when he saw 6 to 8 greenish lights flying uniformly. Some books describe them as yellow lights, as he is still alive, he could clarify the point. He pointed these out to his family and they all watched this wondering if this was one large object with lighted windows or separate smaller craft. He commented that in thousands of hours of sky watching he had never seen anything as strange and they made no sound. This occurred in 1969, no date or month given, and no estimation of height or size, so rather a disappointing report from a top astronomer.

No doubt our present day astronomers also observe UFOs, but with so much man made junk littering the atmosphere above our planet, such as defunct satellites, and debris from them which floats a few miles up or comes into the gravity pull and falls to Earth, then again there are proto-type military secret craft, which no one knows about, so it is small wonder that astronomers and Observatories as a whole, are not prepared to stick their necks out and say they have observed anything strange and unaccountable to them.

In the late 1890's literally thousands of Americans right across the United States collectively saw what appeared to be prototype zeppelin or airships in Illinois, Iowa, Michigan, Nebraska, Winsconsin. This preceded by a few years the first air balloons, or the Wright brothers clumsy first though historic flight. The archives of American newspapers in New York are full of these reports. I suggest people should borrow from their Libraries the books of Charles Fort that great American writer of mysteries of the unknown.

The first air balloon went from St. Cloud round the Eiffel Tower of Paris in 1901. In October 1907 a British airship journeyed slowly from Farnborough, Kent to round St. Paul's Cathedral, London to Crystal Palace, Surrey about 50 miles in three hours 35 mins. So these were clearly not the air ships seen in America neither in 1898, nor in New Zealand and Britain for a few weeks in 1909, when there were hundreds of eyewitness reports of airships neither of these countries possessed.

In 1931 Sir Francis Chichester the famous yachtsman was making a flight in a Moth plane across the Tasman Sea from New South Wales Australia to New Zealand, in an open cockpit. Suddenly he saw a dull grey white craft approaching him, it was pear shaped and flashing brightly, periodically it vanished, and then reappeared beside him, until it finally accelerated away and disappeared into the sea mists.[12]

Some famous people who have seen UFOs in our present time, and have not been afraid to say so, are to be commended. I would enjoin everyone who has seen something unexplainable in the sky, to be sensible and do so as well, people like Stephen Spielberg and lately some television companies are helping to change the climate of thinking, eventually sheer force of public opinion, will collectively make the Governments of this world tell the truth and what they know about the UFO phenomena, for this is something that vitally concerns every single person on this Earth.

Astronauts James Lovell, Edwin Aldrin, Stafford and Cernan, Goredon Cooper and Ed Mitchell and Neil Armstrong, the 1st man on the Moon all saw unexplainable things. They reported them to their cost. Dr. Stanton Friedman nuclear physicist U.S.A., Dr. Felix Ziegel Professor of higher mathematics and astronomy USSR, Dr. Alan Hynek Professor of Astronomy and Head later of UFO World Studies at Evanston, Illinois USA all braved losing their high positions to speak out. Amongst show business people David Icke and Reg Presley spring to mind, Bernie Winters and Michael Bentine the comedians. Shirley Maclaine and quite a number of other show business personalities and pop stars risked ridicule to tell the truth.

They should take heart, the King of all actors and writers William Shakespeare no less, himself recorded a Sighting of three discs of light merging into a Mother craft in King Henry VI Part III Act II, Scene I. (A Plain New Mortimer's Cross, Herefordshire). People today often report small planetary probes entering a far larger and usually very much higher in the sky, Mother craft or Space Craft. Surely it is these and not the many smaller Objects my Witnesses and I have seen that traverse Space?

Of course the bible is peppered with UFO reports, if one looks at these accounts in the light of our present day knowledge. Zechariah writes of a flying roll 'the length thereof is twenty cubits, and the breath thereof ten cubits'. In the book of Ezekiel, an aerial craft lands and the Beings command Ezekiel to give communications to his people. Enoch 'walked with God' and was taken by angels on trips through the Universe, just as many people report today. Abraham entertained three angels, but they broke bread and drank with him, so surely they were not spirits?

All these biblical characters also lived a huge span of years, three to four hundred years, and this was after the fall of Adam and Eve, when mankind was then supposed to live only three score years and ten. Were these in fact Space people? I should like to point out that as far as we know, only Adam and Eve fell from Grace and into original sin. Why should we not suppose that the Beings from other planets still walk in the Grace, wisdom and knowledge of God and therefore compared with the peoples of this Earth are indeed angels. It is only a thought of mine, and not a dogmatic theory.

My friend David Medina the author who died on the 28th January 1996 wrote the very well researched God's Weapon. In this he speculates that after receiving the Ten Commandments on Mount Sinai, Moses was given instructions for building an ark to house the two tabernacles of stone. He contends that the arc of the Covenant was no more than a form of nuclear reactor whereby Moses, Aaron and his four sons were required to wear special protective clothing in order to communicate with God [Space Beings?] The High Priests who disregarded these strict instructions of clothing themselves, washing before and after, just fell dead, or were struck with leprosy.

In Elohim's Nursery David Medina (Regency Press 1981) carries this theme through to the story of Lot, the Destruction of Sodom and Gommorrah, The crossing of the lost tribes of Israel through the river Nile. The manna machine.... right through Biblical times. A scholarly piece of work, which must have cost him many years of careful research. In it he speculates on the numbers of times barren women became pregnant after a visit from the 'man of God!' To-day helpless young women all over the world are being abducted into Alien craft and totally against their will are genetically engineered and impregnated. In the 1970s I never wrote down what they said, just listened with sympathy and belief, knowing I would be drummed out of existence by my fellow Ufologist 'experts' had I dared to write about abductions.

Thank heavens for Dr Leo Sprinkle and Professor John E Mack both highly qualified professors and psychiatrists from the Universities of Wyoming and Harvard. Now that these two brave professionals are gradually being accepted by the UFO fraternity, I can write, but no doubt I will be as vigorously decried as Mr Alan Watts the physicist's ideas in UFO Quest.[13] I was pleased to note that my National Chairman Mike Soper, who is no laggard in the intelligence stakes, found this book readable and thought provoking. This is exactly what I found. I have been meeting Mr Watts for many years, and listened to his theories, and they make far more sense to me than the people who are considered 'in fashion' in the Ufology world at the moment.

Fashions of theories and thoughts come and go, but the age old concept that we are not alone in the Universe will prevail, because it is sheer logic and common sense, to realise that even mathematically it would be impossible for our planet to be the only inhabited one in the vastness of creation.

NOTES:

1. *The Coming of the Saucers, Kenneth Arnold & Ray Palmer 1952*

2. *Founding History of BUFORA*

3. *Flying Saucers have Landed, Desmond Leslie, Werner Laurie, London, England, 1953*

4. *Readers Digest Book of Facts 1985*

5. *Warfare in Ancient India, V R Ramchandra Dikehitar, Translated by Chandra Roy 1889, Macmillan & Co 1945*

6. *Readers Digest Dictionary 1984*
   The Flying Saucer Story, Neville Spearman, Brinsley Le Poer Trench 1996

7. *Gervase of Tilbury Bristol account by Don Boys D.D. Arcturua Books NY 1982*

8. *Flying Saucers Uncensored, Harold T. Wilkins, Citadel Press NY 1955*

9. *The Books of Charles Fort, Henry Holt & Co 1941*

10. *Dr. L. Shklovsky in Komolskays Pravda 1959*

11. *Fly Saucers Uncensored, H.T. Wilkins*

12. *Readers Digest Dictionary/Le Poer Trench, The Sky People*

13. *Alan Watts, UFO Quest, Blandford 1994*
    UFO Visitation, Blandford 1996

As the bulk of this book was completed in 1997 and reviewed by Desmond Leslie that year, the comments, dates and times have been left to 1997.

Recent additions have been -
The Beach, Pensarn, Abergele ref: Pages 57 to 61
The Pentre Halkyn Contactee   ref: Pages 61 to 67

In the intervening years numbers of the people mentioned have since died -
Desmond Leslie who wrote my Foreword, Tim O'Brien, Eileen Morris, my friend and neighbour Mrs Doris Jacques (ref: Page 126) and Mrs Violet Lawrence (ref: Pages 3, 5,8 & 9) died on the 3rd September 2004. I now feel there are hardly any left to collaborate our extraordinary experiences, unless this book finds Miss Deborah de Negri (ref: Pages 4,5,8 & 9)

There are huge losses to the Ufology movement in the death of Gordon Creighton, former Editor of Flying Saucer Review on the 16th July 2003. The untimely passing of Graham W. Birdsall on the 19th September 2003. Professor John E. Mack who was fatally knocked down at a pedestrian crossing in London by a drunken lorry driver on the 27th September 2004. Leroy Gordon Cooper the Mercury 7 astronaut who died on the 4th October 2004. Time and again he stated publicly and to the UN that he had filmed UFOs from Gemini 5 space flight and had witnessed them also as a fighter pilot. All these immeasurable losses to our credibility and UFO Research.

Useful addresses I use:-

My Organisation – Contact International U.K
                    P.O. Box 23 Wheatley,Oxon OX33 lFI, England U.K

The fellowship I co-founded – WFIU (Wales Federation of Independent Ufologists)
                    P.O. Box 197, Rhyl, LL18 1AA, North Wales, U.K.

London Office for BUFORA Ltd. London WC1N 3XX. England U.K
Registered Office for BUFORA JOURNAL
BUFORA Ltd 70 High Street, Wingham,Kent CT3 1BJ   England U.K

FSR Publications Ltd (Flying Saucer Review)
Attn: Mr. Howard Rineback, Box 162, High Wycombe,Bucks H13 5DZ England U.K

County Magazines or News Letters :-
Journal of the Phenomena Research Association,
94 The Circle, Sinfin, Derby DE24 9H, England U.K

Southampton News Letter   SUFOG,
25 Weston Grove, Woolston, Southampton,Hampshire SO19 9EE England U.K

Probe International
15 Knaresboro Avenue, Marton, Blackpool, FY3 9QW, England, UK
E-Mail jean.sam@virgin.net (Conferences arranged)

UFO Monitors East Kent
23 Brabner Close, Folkestone, Kent CT18 6LW England U.K

Books -   Send a large self-addressed,stamped envelope to –

Lionel Beer, 115 Hollybush Lane,Hampton,Middlesex TW12 2QY

Jawbone Books, 8 St.Anthony Road, Sheffield S10 1SG. Yorkshire, England U.K

Ms S.R.Stebbing,41 Terminus Drive,Herne Bay,Kent CT6 6BR, England U.K

Midnight Books, The Mount, Ascerton Road, Sidmouth,Devon EX10 9BT, England
U.K

INDEX